Photography by Simon Wheeler

James Martin's

GREAT BRITISH
WINTER
COOKBOOK

MITCHELL BEAZLEY

For my mother, grandmother, Ken Allinson, Fiona, Linda and Mary

Great British Winter by James Martin

First published in Great Britain in 2006 by Mitchell Beazley, an imprint of
Octopus Publishing Group Ltd, 2-4 Heron Quays, London E14 4JP
An Hachette Livre UK Company
www.hachettelivre.co.uk

First published in paperback in 2008

A CIP catalogue record for this book is available from the British Library.

ISBN: 978 1 84533 477 2

Commissioning Editor: Rebecca Spry
Executive Art Editor: Nicky Collings
Design: Grade Design Consultants
Editor: Susan Fleming
Photography: Simon Wheeler
Home Economy: Katherine Ibbs and Karen Taylor
Production: Jane Rogers

Typeset in Foundry Sans
Printed and bound by Toppan in China

James Martin's

GREAT BRITISH WINTER COOKBOOK

CONTENTS

Introduction

THE MAGIC OF CHRISTMAS takes hold of us as kids and never really leaves us. But as a chef, the real magic of winter for me now lies in the food we eat. Salty baked potatoes, warming winter stews, comforting roast beef with Yorkshire pud – you can't beat it! It's not that those winter festivals like Bonfire Night and New Year's Eve have lost their power to excite me, it's just that the thing I like best about them is the food.

Pretty much everything in this book is seasonal, because the joy of having seasons is cooking different ingredients and different types of dishes. So you'll find all your cold-weather favourites like pumpkins, parsnips and potatoes; cod and mussels; pheasant, goose and beef. But for us Brits the winter is also about occasion. Remember the burgers, toffee apples and toasted marshmallows you used to eat on Bonfire Night? Or the sausage rolls and mulled wine you associate with winter parties? It's all in here! I admit that not everything is traditionally British – I've included lots of dishes that we've adopted from abroad over the years.

Of course there's one festivity that's more important than any other in winter. Yes, I'm talking about Christmas. You'll find all your festive favourites in this book, from a couple of alternatives for the roast bird, to the roast potatoes and parsnips, to the bread sauce and cranberry jelly. And there are loads of vegetarian ideas, too! For those of you who fancy indulging in Christmas baking, there are all the recipes you need – the cake, the pudding, the yule log... even traditional mincemeat.

You know I hate the idea of everyone slogging away over a hot stove, so all the food in this book is simple. Happy winter and happy festivities!

STARTERS

Nothing beats a good British soup in the winter. There are loads of fresh ingredients in season, and I particularly love mussels and root veg as a base for soup. But there's nothing wrong with buying some veg frozen – after all, why go without a food like peas for months when it can be frozen so well? Salads make another brilliant winter starter; they're not just for summer, as my recipes prove!

Bacon and Bean Salad

The dressing is the key to this delicious salad. Its texture is a bit like that of a Caesar salad, but less creamy and heavy. It's a pain to remove the shells of broad beans, but it will be worth it. You'll need about 200g (7oz) fresh or frozen large beans to end up with 100g (3½ oz) here.

Serves 4

8 slices dry-cured streaky bacon
   or 10 slices Parma ham
50g fresh white bread, crusts
   removed, cubed
a knob of unsalted butter
150g (5½oz) mixed red and white
   chicory and rocket
100g (3½oz) cooked French
   beans 100g (3½oz) podded,
   blanched and peeled broad
   beans
5g (⅛oz) fresh flat-leaf parsley,
   picked and washed
extra virgin olive oil
Parmesan shavings (optional)

DRESSING
2 slices white bread, crusts
   removed
4 tbsp milk
juice and finely grated zest of
   1 lemon
2 garlic cloves, peeled
140g (5oz) fresh shelled walnuts
150ml (5fl oz) extra virgin olive oil
salt and freshly ground black
   pepper

1   To make the dressing, tear the bread into the blender and moisten with the milk. Add the lemon zest and juice, garlic and walnuts and blend to a paste. Add, and blend in, the olive oil and some salt and pepper to taste.

2   Grill the bacon or Parma ham until crisp. Fry the cubed bread in a little butter until golden brown.

3   Place the salad leaves and the beans into a bowl. Add the dressing and some salt and pepper and mix.

4   Place a portion of the salad on each plate and top with the crisp bacon, the parsley and croûtons. Drizzle with olive oil and top with the Parmesan shavings.

Lamb, Aubergine and Watercress Salad

A salad in winter? I know what you're thinking, but this one is great: charred aubergine (which we Brits have come to love) served warm with roast loin of lamb. I put watercress and coriander in the salad with red onions, but spring onions will work well, too. The lamb comes from the best end, which has been removed from the bone and trimmed down.

Serves 6

1 x 600g (1lb 5oz) lamb loin, trimmed of fat and silver skin
olive oil
salt and freshly ground black pepper
2 small aubergines, cut into 1.5cm (⅝in) slices

BALSAMIC VINAIGRETTE
4 tbsp balsamic vinegar
1 garlic clove, peeled and finely chopped
a pinch of caster sugar
125ml (4fl oz) olive oil
2 fresh thyme sprigs, leaves picked and washed

WATERCRESS SALAD
100g (3½oz) watercress, stems removed
25g (1oz) fresh coriander, leaves picked
1 red chilli, seeded and cut into strips
1 red onion, peeled and sliced
rind of ½ salted lemon or preserved lemon, cut into strips

1 Preheat the oven to 220°C/425°F/gas mark 7.

2 Brush the lamb with olive oil and season with salt and pepper. Heat a frying pan over a high heat and seal the lamb on all sides until browned. Transfer the lamb to a baking tray and roast for 6-8 minutes for medium. Set aside to rest for 5 minutes before slicing.

3 Preheat an overhead grill or ridged cast-iron grill to a high heat. Lightly brush the aubergine with olive oil and cook for 5-8 minutes, or until tender and browned. Keep warm.

4 Meanwhile, to make the balsamic vinaigrette, whisk all the ingredients together until combined. Season to taste with salt and pepper.

5 To make the salad, combine the watercress, coriander, chilli, onion and lemon rind. Add enough balsamic vinaigrette to moisten it.

6 To serve, place 2-3 slices of aubergine on each serving plate. Slice the lamb loin into discs, about 5mm (¼in) thick, and toss through the salad. Arrange the salad over the aubergine. Finish with a further light drizzle of balsamic vinaigrette.

Baked Crab with a Cheesy Crust

There's a great supplier called Nobles in Whitby. In high season they are knocking out 1,000-plus crabs a day, and not just cooking them but dressing them as well. Their hands are like iron as they rip the shells away while picking the meat out. Crabs are far better than lobsters for flavour and value, and they are much easier to get hold of too.

Serves 4

meat from 4 freshly cooked crabs
25g (1oz) unsalted butter, melted
juice of ½ lemon
1 tsp English mustard
salt and freshly ground black
    pepper
a pinch of medium curry powder
15g (½oz) fresh white
    breadcrumbs
25g (1oz) Parmesan, freshly grated

TO SERVE
1 tbsp balsamic vinegar
3 tbsp extra virgin olive oil
85g (3oz) mixed salad leaves
1 lemon, cut into wedges

1   Preheat the oven to 220°C/425°F/gas mark 7.

2   Mix the brown and white crab-meat in a bowl. Stir in the melted butter, lemon juice and mustard, and season with salt and pepper to taste. Divide this mixture among the crab shells. Place the shells on a baking sheet.

3   Mix the remaining dry ingredients and sprinkle over the crab-meat. Bake until golden, about 6-8 minutes.

4   Combine the vinegar and oil with a little salt and pepper and use this to dress the salad leaves. Serve the crab and salad with lemon wedges.

Drop the live crab into plenty of cold salted water. Bring to the boil.

Simmer for 15 minutes for smaller crabs; 20-25 minutes for larger ones.

Mussel and Saffron Soup with Caramelized Onions and Garlic Croûtons

This cheap soup has great strong flavours, but go carefully; a common mistake is to use too much saffron, as it takes a while to get the right colour and flavour. The soup goes well with the caramelized onions, which I like to make loads of at a time – I also use it on sandwiches and with cheese, especially Cheddar.

Serves 6

50 black mussels, scrubbed and
  bearded (discard any that do
  not close when tapped)
75ml (2½fl oz) dry white wine
1 tbsp olive oil
2 tsp minced garlic
a pinch of crushed red pepper
  flakes
½ small onion, peeled and
  chopped
1 tsp tomato purée
200ml (7fl oz) double cream,
  whipped
500ml (18fl oz) fresh chicken stock
1 tsp saffron strands
1 tbsp chopped fresh chives
salt and freshly ground black
  pepper

CARAMELIZED ONIONS
2 tbsp unsalted butter
2 onions, peeled, halved and thinly
  sliced

1 Caramelize the onions first. Melt the butter in a medium sauté pan over a low heat. Add the onions and sauté until caramel-brown, about 30 minutes, stirring occasionally.

2 To make the soup, combine the mussels and wine in a large, heavy pot over a high heat. Cover and cook, shaking the pot occasionally, until the mussels open, about 4-5 minutes. Discard any mussels that do not open. Drain, reserving the mussel liquor. Shell 40 of the mussels. Strain the reserved mussel liquor through a fine sieve.

3 In a large saucepan over a medium heat, heat the olive oil, and sauté the garlic and pepper flakes until the garlic is light brown. Add the chopped onion and sauté until tender, about 5 minutes. Add the reserved mussel liquor, the tomato purée, cream and stock. Bring to a boil and skim off any foam that develops.

4 Lower the heat, add the saffron and simmer for 5 minutes. Add the shelled mussels and the chives, and season with salt and pepper. Liquidize.

5 To serve, place a spoonful of caramelized onions in the centre of each bowl and scatter a few mussels around in their shells. Then pour the soup over the lot.

Rich Onion Soup with Cheese Toasts

The start of this recipe is most important. The knack of making a good onion soup is colouring the onions well first, as this will give flavour and a deep colour to the finished dish. No gravy browning – that's cheating!

Serves 6

5 onions, peeled and thinly sliced
3 garlic cloves, peeled and
   thinly sliced
20g (³/₄oz) duck fat
300ml (10fl oz) red wine
150ml (5fl oz) fresh beef stock
50ml (2fl oz) brandy
100ml (3¹/₂fl oz) good balsamic
   vinegar
salt and freshly ground black
   pepper
10g (¹/₄oz) fresh flat-leaf parsley
55g (2oz) unsalted butter

CHEESE TOASTS
8 thick slices white bread
280g (10oz) Gruyère cheese

1 Sauté the onion and garlic in a large pan in the duck fat for about 20-30 minutes, colouring very well.

2 Stir before adding the red wine and stock. Bring to the boil and simmer for about 10 minutes. Add the brandy and balsamic vinegar and simmer for another 20 minutes.

3 Preheat the grill well. Toast the bread on both sides, top with the grated cheese and place under the grill to melt.

4 Season the soup well with salt and pepper and add the chopped fresh parsley. Pour into soup bowls. Top with the grilled cheese toasts and a knob of butter.

Roast Tomato and Cumin Soup

Roasting veg for soups, as I've done here and in the squash soup on page 94, makes the soup taste even better. Remember that it's winter, and English toms aren't around, so this is a good way of bringing flavour to imported ones. Serve with thick slices of crusty bread.

Serves 6-8

1.25kg (2¾lb) ripe tomatoes
6 tbsp olive oil
2 medium onions, peeled and
    roughly chopped
3 garlic cloves, peeled and
    roughly chopped
1 large fresh red chilli pepper,
    chopped
2 tbsp cumin seeds, roasted and
    ground
500ml (18fl oz) tomato passata
salt and freshly ground black
    pepper

1   Preheat the oven to 170°C/325°F/gas mark 3.

2   Slice the tomatoes in half and place them on a large, heavy baking sheet. Sprinkle over 2 tbsp of the olive oil and roast for about 1 hour, or until the tomatoes are dehydrated and have caramelized. Remove the tomatoes from the baking sheet and set aside.

3   Place the onion, garlic and chilli in a large saucepan with the remaining olive oil. Cook over a low heat, stirring occasionally, until the onion is soft and translucent, about 10 minutes. Add the cumin and fry for another 5 minutes. Add the roasted tomatoes and the tomato passata and cook for 10 minutes.

4   Purée the mixture in a food processor or blender.

5   To serve, transfer the mixture back into a saucepan and reheat gently until warm. Taste and add salt and pepper as desired. Ladle into warm bowls. Serve with some charred ciabatta.

Pea Soup

I was brought up on this, and I love it! My gran used to put chunks of leftover ham with the bone in this soup, which adds extra flavour. I like it with fresh mint leaves thrown in at the end. But soups can be easily overcooked and none more so than this: the last thing you want is a wrinkly bullet in the bottom of your soup bowl.

Serves 6-8

1 bunch spring or young green-
  stemmed onions, chopped
2 garlic cloves, peeled and chopped
25g (1oz) unsalted butter
600g (1lb 5oz) podded young peas
675g (1½lb) leftover cooked/
  boiled ham, roughly chopped
600ml (1 pint) fresh chicken stock
250ml (9fl oz) double cream
  (optional)
salt and ground black pepper
1 mint sprig (8-12 leaves), chopped

1 Sweat the onion and garlic in the butter in a covered pan for 5 minutes, without colouring.

2 Add the peas, ham and stock, and bring to the boil. If using the cream, add now and simmer until the peas are tender, about 10 minutes.

3 Season to taste, and liquidize if you like, adding another 25g (1oz) butter. But why bother blending? I think it looks and tastes so much better when you can see the bits of food you're eating (and without the extra cream). Serve sprinkled with the mint.

Sweetcorn and Crab Soup

This may be taking its place in a British cookbook, but the idea came from one of the Indian chefs in my restaurant. Yuri makes great soup, and this is one of my favourites.

Serves 6

1 large white onion, peeled
250g (9oz) potatoes, peeled
curry powder
30g (1¼oz) unsalted butter
1.2 litres (2 pints) chicken stock
handful of fresh basil leaves
300ml (10fl oz) double cream
450g (1lb) frozen sweetcorn
  kernels
meat from 2 freshly cooked crabs
olive oil

1 Dice the onion and potatoes. In a large, heavy pan, sweat them with curry powder to taste in the butter until soft. Pour in the stock, stir, and bring to the boil, then simmer until the potato is tender, about 15 minutes.

2 Meanwhile, whizz most of the basil in a blender until finely chopped. Add 250ml (9fl oz) of the double cream and mix. Season and chill.

3 Add the sweetcorn to the soup, simmer for 3 minutes, then add the crabmeat and remove from the heat. Purée while still hot, then return to the pan, add the remaining cream, and simmer for 3 minutes. Season. Spoon into bowls. Add a little basil cream and olive oil and a basil leaf.

Smoked Haddock Risotto with Saffron, Peas and Grilled Fennel

I love to give an unusual twist to a great British classic – and here's my version of that Brit favourite, smoked haddock soup. It's ideal for those cool days when autumn is turning into winter and fennel is in season.

Serves 4 as a main,
8 as a starter

750g (1lb 10oz) undyed smoked haddock
about 1.2 litres (40fl oz) fresh fish or vegetable stock
2 fennel bulbs, trimmed and sliced
1 small white onion, peeled and sliced
85g (3oz) unsalted butter
450g (1lb) arborio rice
100ml (3½fl oz) white wine
a pinch of saffron strands
140g (5oz) Parmesan, grated
175g (6oz) frozen peas
10g (¼oz) mixed fresh parsley and coriander leaves
85g (3oz) mascarpone cheese
salt and freshly ground black pepper
1 lemon, cut into wedges

1 Skin the haddock and pick over to remove any bones. Cut the fish into dice. Heat the stock on top of the stove.

2 Put half of the fennel slices and all the onion slices in a suitable pan with the butter and cook for about 3 minutes. Add the rice and cook for a further minute. Add the wine and saffron and stir until the wine has been absorbed.

3 Gradually add ladlefuls of the hot stock, stirring, and waiting until the stock has been absorbed by the rice before adding any more. After about 10 minutes, add the diced haddock and continue to cook until the rice is tender, about another 5 minutes.

4 Meanwhile, grill the remaining fennel slices until tender and golden, about 3-4 minutes.

5 Add the Parmesan, peas, herbs and mascarpone to the risotto and stir to heat the peas through. Season to taste. Serve the risotto with the grilled fennel on top, and a wedge of lemon to the side.

Thai Chicken Cakes with Sweet Chilli Sauce

I know these little cakes aren't classically British, but we love them don't we? They make a great starter or snack. If you want to cool the sauce down for the kids, mix it with a little crème fraîche. You can also place the chicken mixture on skewers – it looks great.

Serves 4 as a starter

2 chicken breasts, skinned and cubed
1 garlic clove, peeled and roughly chopped
1 x 1cm (½ in) knob fresh root ginger, peeled and chopped
1 small onion, peeled and roughly chopped
2 tbsp chopped fresh coriander
1 green chilli, roughly chopped
salt and freshly ground black pepper
2 tbsp olive oil

CHILLI SAUCE
55g (2oz) caster sugar
2 red chillies, chopped
1 tomato, chopped
4 Kaffir lime leaves
2 lemongrass stalks, finely chopped
25g (1oz) fresh root ginger, peeled and chopped
2 garlic cloves, peeled and chopped
1 shallot, peeled and chopped
2 tbsp fish sauce
25ml (1fl oz) sesame oil
50ml (2fl oz) dark soy sauce
2 tbsp clear honey
juice and finely grated zest of 2 limes

TO SERVE
4 spring onions, trimmed and finely sliced

1 To make the chilli sauce place the sugar in a pan on a medium heat and heat gently to a caramel colour. Don't let it burn.

2 Meanwhile, purée all the rest of the sauce ingredients in a blender. Pour into the caramel-coloured sugar and stir well. Bring to the boil and cook for about 5 minutes, simmering gently. Allow to cool, season with salt and pepper and chill in the fridge.

3 Place the chicken, garlic, ginger, onion, coriander and chilli in a food processor and season to taste with salt and pepper. Blitz for 15-20 seconds. Shape the chicken mixture into small cakes.

4 Heat the olive oil in a frying pan over a moderate heat and fry the chicken cakes until golden on both sides and cooked through, about 3-4 minutes in total.

5 Serve immediately, with the sweet chilli sauce and spring onions.

MEAT AND GAME BIRDS

We Brits produce some really great meat, so why mess about with it?
Simple terrines and great roasts with all the trimmings helped to build our
nation! I really believe in using the whole animal; I used to love watching
my grandad carefully fry calves' liver.

Fillet of Beef with Prune and Potato Cakes

For my college exam in the early 1990s, I had to make a classic potato dish call Pommes Anna, which is a layered cake of potatoes and butter cooked in a mould. It's a pain in the backside to make and was a pretty pointless exercise as I've never made it since. However, people love rösti, which is made with grated spuds, and this is a mixture of the two.

Serves 4

4 x 200g (7oz) fillet steaks
25g (1oz) unsalted butter
extra virgin olive oil
1 small white onion, peeled
    and diced
2 garlic cloves, peeled
    and chopped
200g (7oz) fresh chanterelle
    mushrooms, washed and dried
2 tomatoes, diced
5g (1/8 oz) fresh parsley leaves,
    chopped
salt and freshly ground black
    pepper
85g (3 oz) washed and destemmed
    spinach leaves

RED WINE SAUCE
1/2 red onion, peeled and chopped
2 tbsp extra virgin olive oil
750ml (1 pint 7fl oz) fresh beef
    stock
1/3 bottle red wine
10g (1/4 oz) unsalted butter

PRUNE AND POTATO CAKE
450g (1lb) baking potatoes
100g (3 1/2 oz) unsalted butter,
    melted
8 fresh prunes, stoned and
    chopped

1   Preheat the oven to 200°C/400°F/gas mark 6. To make the red wine sauce, sauté the onion in the oil until it has softened, about 2 minutes, then add the stock and red wine. Bring to the boil, then simmer to reduce to a good sauce consistency. Pass through a sieve, add the butter, and keep warm to one side.

2   For the potato cakes, peel and sculpt the potatoes into barrel shapes. Slice very thinly on a mandolin. Mix the slices with the melted butter and season with salt and pepper.

3   Using 4 holes of a 6-hole Yorkshire pudding tin, or 4 x 7.5cm (3in) non-stick tins, layer the potato, about 4 slices thick, and then add a few chopped prunes. Top with the same amount of potatoes again. Don't worry if the potato is higher than the tins; it will collapse while cooking. Bake for 30 minutes, then remove from the oven and allow to cool. Remove from the tins and keep to one side, leaving the oven on.

4   Meanwhile, cook the fillets. Heat up a shallow frying pan on the stove and place the seasoned fillets in the dry pan. Colour well on one side before turning over and adding half the butter and the same amount of olive oil.

5   In a separate pan, sauté the onion, garlic and chanterelles in the remaining butter, then add 200ml (7fl oz) of the red wine sauce (if you have any left over, reserve it for use another time), the tomatoes and chopped parsley. Season to taste.

6   To serve, wilt the spinach in a pan with just the water clinging to the leaves. Drain the spinach well, then place on the plates, top with a potato cake and then a steak. Finish by spooning the sauce and mushrooms over the top.

Peppered Roast Beef

Do I have to say anything? Just look at it and eat it! The Yorkshire has loads of eggs in it, but it works – *if* you place the mix in hot tins, *if* you leave the oven door closed and *if* you make the mixture in advance and leave it to rest. This is the best recipe for Yorkies I've ever tasted. If I can't make Yorkshire pud coming from where I do, then I should shoot myself!

Serves 8

1 x 6-rib joint of beef
salt and freshly ground black
   pepper
cooking fat or oil
1 large fresh rosemary sprig,
   leaves picked

1   Preheat the oven to 220°C/425°F/gas mark 7. Season the beef with plenty of pepper and a sprinkle of salt.

2   Heat some oil or fat in a hot roasting pan, then add the meat to seal. Remove from the heat, sprinkle with rosemary leaves, and place in the oven. A joint of this size will take 1½-2 hours to cook, but this depends on how you like to eat it. Cooking for 1 hour will keep it rare; 2 hours, medium; 2½ hours, medium-to-well-done.

3   Once cooked, leave the meat to rest for 15-20 minutes before carving. This will relax the meat, and it will become even more tender. Serve with Yorkshire pudding (below), roast potatoes and perhaps parsnips (*see* page 131) and gravy.

Yorkshire Pudding

Serves 4

225g (8oz) plain flour
salt and freshly ground black
   pepper
8 medium free-range eggs
600ml (1 pint) milk
55g (2oz) good dripping or 50ml
   (2fl oz) vegetable oil

1   Place the flour and some seasoning in a bowl and make a well in the middle. Add the eggs one by one, using a whisk, then whisk in the milk, mixing very well until the batter is smooth and there are no lumps. Leave in the fridge for at least an hour or, even better, overnight. Preheat the oven to about 220°C/425°F/gas mark 7.

2   Divide the dripping or oil among 8 Yorkshire pudding tins (13cm/5in in diameter) or 12 muffin tins, and place in the oven to get very hot.

3   Carefully remove the trays from the oven and, with a ladle or a jug, fill the tins with the batter and place back in the oven immediately. Cook for about 20 minutes before opening the door to check – otherwise they will collapse. If undercooked, reduce the heat to 200°C/400°F/gas mark 6 and cook for a further 10-15 minutes. Serve immediately

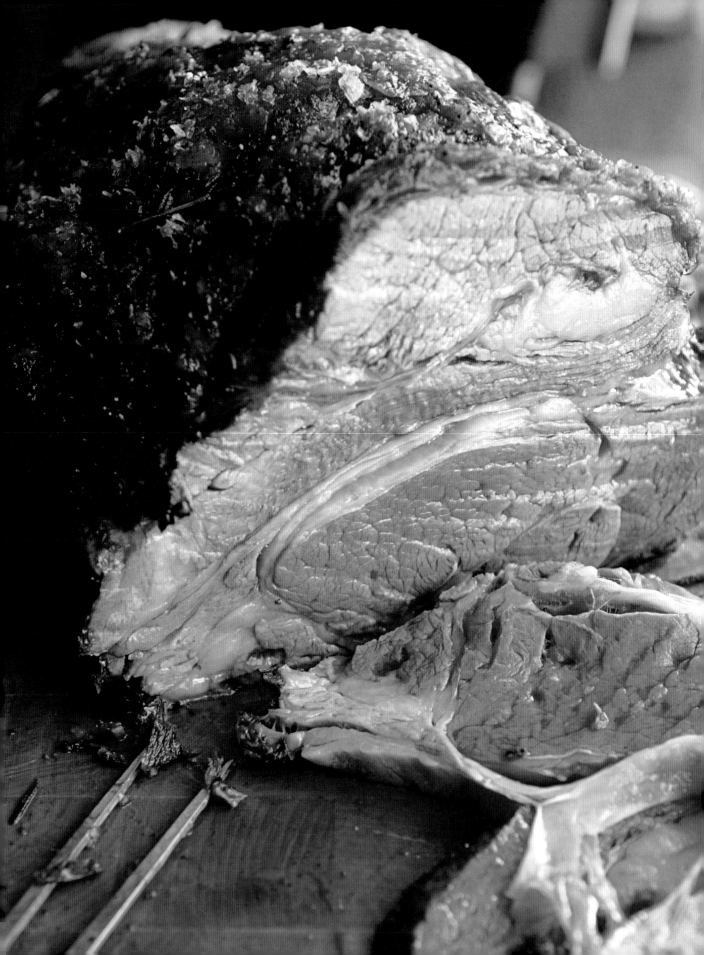

Pork Terrine with Apricots and Pistachios

Good sausages are used as the base of this simple terrine. You could play around with the flavours by using beef or game sausages instead of pork. I've used plum sauce, as this combines with the orange segments to give a sweet-and-sour flavour. When making terrines, make sure you don't overcook them or they will break up while being sliced.

Serves 8-12

olive oil
250g (9 oz) streaky bacon rashers
900g (2lb) or 14-15 large sausages
   (Lincolnshire are best)
10 fresh sage leaves, chopped
5g (1/8 oz) fresh flat-leaf parsley,
   chopped
100g (3 1/2 oz) dried apricots,
   chopped
75g (2 3/4 oz) shelled pistachio
   nuts, roughly chopped
salt and freshly ground black
   pepper

SALAD

2 oranges, peeled and segmented
55g (2 oz) wild rocket leaves
1 large potato, peeled, cooked
   and diced
8 tbsp plum sauce (make your
   own, or buy the Chinese stuff
   from the supermarket)
3 tbsp olive oil

1 Preheat the oven to 180°C/350°F/gas mark 4. Take a terrine dish, 30-35cm (12-14in) long, 10cm (4in) wide, and 9-10cm (3 1/2-4 in) deep, and brush it with olive oil. Line the dish with streaky bacon, leaving 5-6cm (2-2 1/2 in) overlapping the edge of the terrine.

2 Make the filling by removing all the meat from the sausage skins (discard these). Add the sage, parsley, chopped apricots and pistachio nuts and mix well with plenty of seasoning.

3 Pile the meat mixture into the terrine mould and press down well. Fold over the bacon and either cover with the lid or with foil, and place in a bain-marie half-filled with hot water. Cook in the oven for 60 minutes. Remove from the oven, cover with foil, and press down with a weight. Cool, then place in the fridge.

4 When ready to serve, make the salad by mixing the orange segments, rocket and potato together in a bowl. Mix the plum sauce with the olive oil and seasoning to taste.

5 Cut the terrine into slices and serve in the centre of the plates with the salad around and the dressing spooned over the top.

Yorkshire Ham Terrine with Spiced Pickle

Scotts butchers in York is still the best place to buy Yorkshire gammon and ham, but if you visit you have to queue. Last time I was there it was obviously pension day, as the place was like a gala bingo hall on a jackpot night.

Serves 10

3 ham knuckles
4 bay leaves
6 black peppercorns
1 large onion, peeled and halved
1 medium leek, halved
1 medium carrot, peeled and halved
extra virgin olive oil
6-8 thin slices York ham, or other cooked sliced ham
2 shallots, peeled and finely chopped
1 garlic clove, peeled
salt and freshly ground black pepper
20g (³/₄oz) fresh parsley leaves, finely chopped
a pinch of ground mixed spice
2 gelatine leaves, soaked in cold water for 5 minutes
55g (2oz) mixed salad leaves and herbs (chervil, wild rocket, etc)

PINEAPPLE PICKLE
1 garlic clove, peeled and crushed
1 tsp grain mustard
5 tbsp white wine vinegar
a good pinch of turmeric powder
150g (5¹/₂oz) demerara sugar
1 medium pineapple, skinned, cored and finely chopped

DRESSING
4 tbsp each of grain mustard, extra virgin olive oil and cider vinegar

1 Put the ham knuckles, bay leaves, peppercorns, onion, leek and carrot in a large saucepan. Cover with cold water, bring to the boil and simmer, covered, for 3 hours, until the meat is tender.

2 Meanwhile, grease a 20 x 8cm (8 x 3 ¹/₄in) terrine mould with olive oil. Line with clingfilm, then with the sliced York ham.

3 When the ham knuckles are nearly cooked, heat a little olive oil in a small pan and gently sweat the shallots and whole garlic clove.

4 Remove the cooked ham knuckles from the pan, reserving the stock, and leave to cool slightly. While warm, remove the meat in pieces from the bone. Place in a small bowl with the shallot and garlic, some salt and pepper and the parsley. Mix well, then pack into the terrine mould.

5 Strain the ham stock. Taste and, if it is too salty, dilute with water. Pour 500ml (18fl oz) into a pan and add the mixed spice. Warm gently and add the soaked gelatine; leave for 2-3 minutes for the gelatine to dissolve before stirring. Pour into the terrine and overlap the edges of the ham. Cover with clingfilm; the terrine needs to be quite solid and "packed". Put a uniform weight on the terrine to press it down (I use a brick) and leave overnight in the fridge.

6 To make the pickle, put all the ingredients together in a pan except for the pineapple. Simmer for 3 minutes, then add the pineapple and cook for a further 3 minutes. Put into sterilized jars and cool.

7 To make the mustard seed dressing, whisk all the ingredients together, then use some of it to dress the salad leaves at the last minute.

8 To serve, turn out the terrine and remove the clingfilm. Using a sharp knife, cut into 2cm (³/₄in) slices and place a slice in the centre of each plate. On each plate, spoon a pile of pineapple pickle, placing a few dressed leaves on, too. Grind over a little black pepper, and serve.

Pot-roast Pheasant with Cider and Calvados

While doing the photography for this book I went shooting at Jody Schekter's farm up the road from me. It was a great day and, as usual, the number of birds we said we shot was different to the number we took home. Typical men, I know! If you buy a brace of birds, or a cock and a hen, remember hens are smaller so will need to be removed before the cocks.

Serves 4

55g (2oz) butter
2 pheasants, cleaned
salt and freshly ground black
 pepper
1 onion, finely chopped
85g (3oz) bacon lardons
1 stick celery, chopped
1 carrot, peeled and chopped
4 sprigs sage
2 Granny Smith apples, peeled,
 cored and cut into large chunks
50ml (2fl oz) calvados
500ml (18fl oz) dry cider
290ml (½ pint) chicken stock
290ml (½ pint) double cream

BAKED APPLES
4 Cox's apples, peeled and cored
25g (1oz) melted butter
1 tbsp soft light brown sugar

TO SERVE
deep-fried sage leaves
8 slices of crispy cooked pancetta
kale, blanched

1 Preheat oven to 190°C/375°F/gas mark 5. Melt the butter in a large non-stick casserole pot. Season the pheasants with salt and ground black pepper. Place the pheasants into the casserole pot and brown until pale golden on all sides. Remove from the pot and set aside.

2 Add the onion, bacon, celery, carrot and sage sprigs to the pot and cook over a medium heat until the onion is soft and translucent and the bacon is crispy. Carefully pour off any excess fat from the lardons.

3 Return the pheasants to the pot and scatter over the apples. Pour over most of the calvados and set alight. Once the flames have died down, add 290ml (½ pint) of the cider and the chicken stock. Bring to a gentle simmer, cover and place in the oven for about 20 minutes, until the birds are cooked through.

4 For the baked apples, place the apples on a baking tray that has been brushed with a little butter and sprinkle with the sugar. Bake for about ½ hour, basting the apples a few times during cooking.

5 Remove the pheasants from the pot and place on a chopping board. Remove the thighs and breasts and set aside to keep warm. Chop the carcass into 4 pieces and place them back in the pot with the vegetables with the remaining cider. Bring to a boil and simmer gently for 5 minutes.

6 Strain the sauce into a bowl through a fine-meshed sieve. Pour the strained sauce back into the pot and add a splash of calvados. Reduce by half. Add the cream and simmer for a further 5 minutes, or until the sauce is creamy and slightly thickened. Return the pheasant breasts and thighs to the pot to warm through and become coated in the sauce.

7 Remove the baked apples from the oven. Serve the pheasant on a bed of kale with a baked apple. Garnish with deep-fried sage leaves and crispy pancetta.

Honey-roast Duck Confit with Tomato Beans

I made this dish up while doing a dinner party in Scotland, and it's now a favourite. Canned beans and canned tomatoes can taste great heated together as we all know – think of beans on toast – but this goes to another level.

Serves 4

4 duck legs
fine salt and freshly ground black
   pepper
2-3 fresh thyme sprigs, leaves
   picked off
300g (10½oz) duck fat
2 tbsp clear honey

TOMATO BEANS
4 tbsp extra virgin olive oil
1 white onion, peeled and
   finely chopped
4 garlic cloves, peeled and
   finely chopped
100ml (3 ½fl oz) white wine
2 fresh thyme sprigs
1 x 400g can chopped tomatoes
6 medium tomatoes
1 x 350g can flageolet beans,
   drained and rinsed
55g (2oz) unsalted butter
10g (¼oz) fresh parsley, chopped

RED WINE SAUCE
½ red onion, peeled and chopped
2 tbsp extra virgin olive oil
750ml (1 pint 7fl oz) fresh beef
   stock
⅓ bottle red wine
10g (¼oz) unsalted butter

1   To make the duck confit, weigh the legs, then put them on a small tray. Sprinkle with 15g (½oz) salt per kg, and the fresh thyme leaves. Cover with clingfilm and place in the fridge overnight.

2   Remove the legs from the tray, wipe off the salt, and put them in a frying pan with the duck fat. Cook slowly, covered, for about 2½ hours, turning occasionally. Leave to cool in the fat.

3   When you are about half an hour from serving, preheat the oven to 180°C/350°F/gas mark 4.

4   To make the beans, heat the olive oil in a pan and sauté the onion and garlic for a few minutes. Add the wine, thyme and tomatoes, both canned and fresh, and bring to a simmer. After 15 minutes, add the beans and simmer for a further 15 minutes. Season with salt and pepper, and add the butter and parsley to finish. Keep warm.

5   To make the red wine sauce, sauté the onion in the oil until it is softened, about 2 minutes, then add the stock and red wine. Bring to the boil, then simmer to reduce to a good sauce consistency. Pass through a sieve, add the butter, and keep warm to one side.

6   Meanwhile, scrape the fat from the duck legs and place in a roasting pan. Smear the honey over the duck legs, then roast for 20 minutes, spooning the honey glaze over the legs at least a couple of times, until cooked through.

7   To serve, place the beans on the plates and top with the duck confit. Spoon the sauce around.

Duck Liver Pâté with Pear Chutney

I hated liver as a kid, as most kids do. The only two dishes my grandad would cook were calves' liver and poached haddock. I used to watch him with his Brylcreemed stick-back hair as he pan-fried his slice of liver with precision. He never failed to try to get me to eat some as I ran out of the door in horror. I now know I was missing out on something great.

Serves 14-16

1kg (2¼lb) organic duck livers, left whole, but all green and thready bits removed
Cognac
2 garlic cloves, peeled and finely chopped
a handful of fresh basil leaves
salt and freshly ground black pepper
350g (12oz) unsalted butter

GARNISH
brown bread, sliced and toasted, or Melba toast
pear chutney
mixed salad leaves, dressed

1 Place the livers in a single layer in a heatproof dish, and scatter over some Cognac. It should not cover them, but they need to wallow in it for several hours. Turn them over so both sides absorb the alcohol. The garlic, all but 2 of the basil leaves (torn and minus the stalks) and some salt and pepper should be thrown into the brew just before poaching.

2 Gently poach the livers, turning them over after a couple of minutes, and continue to stew until they are cooked on the outside but pink within, about 3-4 minutes, until cooked. Do not overcook or you will end up with a drab, brown, crumbly result.

3 Tip the contents of the dish straight into your blender with 225g (8oz) of the softened butter, and whiz until smooth. Check the seasoning, then scrape into a large terrine dish and leave to cool.

4 Meanwhile, clarify the remaining butter. Gently melt it, and pour into another container, leaving behind all the curd-like sediment. Cool a little.

5 Pour the buttercup-coloured clear liquid butter over the surface of the pâté, place the reserved basil leaves in the centre, and put it into the fridge until set.

6 Using a hot knife, slice the terrine. Serve with a slice of toast, a spoonful of chutney and some dressed mixed salad leaves.

VEGETABLES

We have so many fantastic winter veg! Our roots are brilliant, yet we seem to forget about so many of them. Beetroot is a particular favourite of mine, yet loads of people I know don't like it. I reckon if they tried it well cooked they'd quickly change their minds. I recommend growing your own veg – I've just planted my own veg patch in my garden and I can't wait until the new season to try it!

Red Onion and Crème Fraîche Tarts

I use red onions for this instead of Spanish white onions because they require much less cooking and because they start off red, but instantly turn a dark, deep, rich caramel when you add balsamic. I serve this in my restaurant on the ship, and it always proves popular. I've just planted red onions in my garden and am looking forward to the new season.

Serves 4

250g (9oz) ready-rolled puff pastry
   (defrosted if frozen)
1 small egg, beaten
salt and freshly ground black
   pepper
100ml (3½fl oz) olive oil, plus
   extra for drizzling
2 tbsp balsamic vinegar
100g (3½oz) fresh rocket leaves

Filling

3 large red onions, peeled and
   thinly sliced
6 garlic cloves, peeled and
   crushed
4 fresh thyme sprigs
25g (1oz) unsalted butter
125g (4½oz) full-fat crème fraîche

1 If using frozen pastry, allow it to defrost. Preheat the oven to 220°C/425°F/gas mark 7. Roll the puff pastry out until it is half as thick as it was when it was opened (about 3mm thick, or as thin as you dare) and cut into 4 round circles the size of a side plate. Using a sharp knife, cut a small, frame-like edge around the whole pastry and lay this, in pieces, around the outer edge of the tarts. Alternatively, make 1 large rectangular tart.

2 Break the egg into a bowl and whisk with a fork. Brush the pastry circles or rectangle around the edges. Dock with a fork before baking for 15-20 minutes, until the pastry is cooked.

3 For the filling, in a large pan fry the onions, garlic and thyme in the butter for 15 minutes, until well caramelized. Season well. Remove the cooked base/s from the oven and spread with the crème fraiche, then top with the caramelized onions, drizzle with olive oil and return to the oven for a few minutes, until cooked.

4 In a bowl, mix the balsamic vinegar with the olive oil and some salt and pepper. Combine the salad leaves with the dressing.

5 Remove the tart/s from the oven and place on a serving plate. Drizzle with a little olive oil and serve with a small pile of the dressed salad in the middle of the tart.

Beetroot and Mascarpone Risotto

A not-so-British dish, but we've come to love risotto and this dish uses my favourite British winter veg – beetroot! Served with salmon and cauliflower in a salad, or simply cooked in a risotto like this, it gives fantastic flavour and is a good way of introducing beetroot to those who think they don't like it. A mate of mine loves this risotto with a seared steak and salad.

Serves 4

6 raw beetroots, peeled and roughly chopped
500ml (18fl oz) fresh vegetable stock
2 garlic cloves, peeled and finely chopped
2 shallots, peeled and finely chopped
2 fresh thyme sprigs
25g (1oz) unsalted butter
225g (8oz) arborio rice
100ml (3½fl oz) white wine
3 tbsp mascarpone cheese
2 tbsp chopped fresh parsley
115g (4oz) Parmesan, freshly grated
salt and freshly ground black pepper

1 Blend the beetroot in the food processor with half the stock and leave it to one side. Have the remaining stock warming in a pan on the stove.

2 Put the garlic, shallot and thyme in a pan in the butter and sweat for about a minute. Add the rice and stir to coat with the butter. Add the wine and cook, stirring, until it evaporates.

3 Add a ladleful of beetroot stock and, stirring continuously, bring to the boil. Once this has been absorbed by the rice, add another ladleful and bring to the boil again. Keep going like this until all the beetroot stock is used up. Then continue the process with the hot vegetable stock. Simmer for about 12 minutes in all, stirring, until the rice is cooked but still has a little bite.

4 Once the rice is cooked, stir in the mascarpone, parsley, Parmesan and salt and pepper. Serve hot.

Salad of Chargrilled Leeks and Red Onions with Mozzarella

The thing I love most about this dish is the dressing; I sometimes serve it with plain little gem lettuce and some croûtons or, even better, warm French beans and seared tuna or salmon. You can change this salad totally by adding smoked chicken or plainly cooked chicken. You don't have to use mozzarella, but you should choose a mild cheese.

Serves 4

a pinch of caster sugar
salt and freshly ground black
    pepper
24 young leeks, trimmed
2 red onions, peeled and cut into
    wedges
2 x 200g mozzarella balls, cut into
    4 slices each

DRESSING
4 tbsp tarragon vinegar
1 tsp Dijon mustard
1 tbsp chopped fresh tarragon
50ml (2fl oz) extra virgin olive oil
1 tomato, seeded and finely diced
1 tbsp fine capers, rinsed and
    drained
1 tbsp stoned green olives, finely
    chopped
1 hard-boiled egg, shelled and
    finely chopped

1   Make the dressing first. Combine all the ingredients and leave for an hour or so for the flavours to come together.

2   Bring a large pan of water to the boil with the sugar and a little salt. Throw in the leeks, return to the boil and cook gently for 2-3 minutes. Drain them well and dry on a cloth.

3   Grill the leeks and onions on a hot, ridged cast-iron griddle pan. When they are tender and slightly blackened, remove from the heat and season with salt and pepper.

4   Toss the leeks and onions in the dressing, then divide among 4 plates. Arrange 2 slices of mozzarella over each portion, and serve.

Roasted Vegetables with Rosemary and Honey

This is a fab way to serve veg if you are doing a dinner party or a Sunday lunch. It's a bucket-load less stressful than five pans of boiling water with overcooked roots inside! Just chop everything up, sprinkle and drizzle, and throw it in the oven.

Serves 6

450g (1lb) new potatoes
450g (1lb) parsnips
450g (1lb) carrots
225g (8oz) fennel bulbs
225g (8oz) red onions
6 tbsp olive oil
75ml (2½fl oz) clear honey
25g (1oz) unsalted butter
1 fresh rosemary sprig, torn into
   4 pieces
salt and freshly ground black
   pepper
1 lemon (optional)

1 Preheat the oven to 220°C/425°F/gas mark 7.

2 Wash the potatoes, parsnips, carrots and fennel, but don't peel them, then slice into large chunky pieces. Cut the red onions into quarters.

3 Place all the vegetables into an oven tray and drizzle with olive oil and honey. Add the butter in knobs and sprinkle on the rosemary. Season well. Roast for 30-40 minutes.

4 Remove from the oven and coat all the vegetables in the glaze in the base of the pan. Serve with some lemon juice squeezed over if you like.

Shallot Tarte Tatin

I love to make classic dishes easy – and this one really is simple. Tarte tatin is French, but over the years we've nicked it, and now it's ours, too!

Serves 4

350g (12oz) shallots, peeled
olive oil
115g (4oz) caster sugar
25g (1oz) unsalted butter
salt and freshly ground black
    pepper
200g (7oz) ready-rolled puff pastry

TO SERVE
225g (8oz) goat's cheese
8 tbsp runny honey
truffle oil
30g (1¼oz) wild rocket leaves

1 Preheat the oven to 200°C/400°F/gas mark 6.

2 Roast the shallots with a little olive oil for 20 minutes.

3 In a clean non-stick ovenproof pan, melt the sugar to a caramel. Add the butter and mix with the caramel. While hot, pour the mixture into 4 x 7.5cm (3in) non-stick Yorkshire pudding tins. Add the roasted shallots until each tin is full and a tight fit. Season with salt and pepper.

4 Cut the puff pastry into 4 circles about 1cm (½in) bigger than the tins. Place the pastry on top of the shallots, and tuck in the edges down the side of the tins to seal in the shallots. Place the tins in the oven and bake for 15 minutes, until the pastry is cooked.

5 Meanwhile, preheat the grill to medium. With a sharp knife, cut the goat's cheese in 1cm (½in) slices.

6 Turn the tarts out, while piping hot, on to an oven tray. Top with slices of goat's cheese and place under the grill for a few minutes to brown the cheese.

7 Meanwhile, mix the honey and a little truffle oil together. Place a tart on each plate and garnish with the rocket dressed with the honey and truffle oil.

Quick Onion Bhajis

This recipe isn't really mine, as it comes from one of my boys in the bistro kitchen. I promised him I'd put them in the book. I hope you like these as much as I do. I know bhajis are not really British, but we've kind of adopted them. To make a good dip for them, mix some ground cumin, lime juice and chopped mint into some Greek yoghurt.

Makes 8-10

2 onions, peeled and thinly sliced
70g (2½oz) self-raising flour
1 tsp medium curry powder
½ tsp ground cumin
2 tsp turmeric powder
½ tsp salt
150ml (5fl oz) plain yoghurt
vegetable oil for deep-frying

1 Place the onions, flour, spices and salt in a bowl and then stir in the plain yoghurt.

2 Divide the mixture into small balls in the palm of your hands.

3 Heat the oil to 180°C/350°F, then deep-fry the bhajis for 1-2 minutes, to colour and cook. Drain on kitchen paper and cool for a while.

4 Serve as required, with either a spiced yoghurt dip (*see* above) or some mango chutney.

Stilton Fondue with Pears and Walnut Bread

If you don't have a fondue, improvise with an oven-to-table dish on a rack over nightlights.

Serves 4

150g (5½oz) Stilton, diced
85g (3oz) mascarpone
75ml (2½fl oz) double cream
a drizzle of vodka
salt and ground black pepper
3 pears, cored and sliced
½ walnut bread loaf, in chunks

1 Place the Stilton, mascarpone and double cream in a pan and warm over a low heat until the cheeses have melted.

2 Add the vodka, remove from the heat and season.

3 Place the pears and bread in separate dishes. Serve the fondue warm in the middle of the table.

Double-baked Cheese Soufflés

I know it doesn't have veg in it, but humour me! This is the ideal centrepiece for vegetarians.

Serves 6

unsalted butter
250g (9oz) ground almonds
40g (1½oz) plain flour
300ml (10fl oz) hot milk
160g (5¾oz) Emmental, grated
5 medium egg yolks
salt and ground black pepper
500ml (18fl oz) egg whites
3 tbsp lemon juice

SAUCE

1.3 litres (2¼ pints) double cream
250ml (9fl oz) kirsch
140g (5oz) Emmental, grated

1 Preheat the oven to 180°C/350°F/gas mark 4. Butter 6 small soufflé moulds, then dust with ground almonds. Put the moulds in a roasting tray.

2 To make the béchamel base of the soufflés, melt 40g (1½oz) butter in a pan, add the flour and stir until smooth. Add the hot milk gradually, stirring, until smooth. While it is still hot, stir in the grated cheese until melted. Leave to cool. Stir in the egg yolks and season.

3 Whisk the egg whites with the lemon juice until firm. Add a quarter of this to the cheese béchamel and fold in. When smooth, slowly fold in the rest. Fill the moulds with this. Pour enough boiling water into the roasting tray to come halfway up the moulds, then put the tray in the oven for 10 minutes. Allow the soufflés to cool. (You could freeze them at this stage). Reduce the oven temperature to 170°C/325°F/gas mark 3.

4 Remove the soufflés from the moulds, and place in a baking dish. For the sauce, mix the cream and kirsch, pour over the soufflés, and top with the grated Emmental. Bake in the cooler oven for 8 minutes. Serve the soufflés hot, with their sauce.

Parsley and Mozzarella Croquettes

Party food without the mess, as the cheese will melt inside – and a great side dish, too.

Makes 24

1kg (2¼lb) potatoes, peeled
a pinch of freshly grated nutmeg
salt and freshly ground black
    pepper
25g (1oz) unsalted butter
200g (7oz) mozzarella, finely diced
2 medium egg yolks
15g (½oz) fresh parsley leaves,
    chopped
plain flour
2 medium eggs, beaten
140g (5oz) fresh white
    breadcrumbs
vegetable oil for deep-frying

1   Place the potatoes in salted water, bring to the boil and simmer until they are tender.

2   Drain and return to the pan. Place over a low heat and mash-fry with a potato masher. Season with the nutmeg, salt and pepper, then beat in the butter and cool.

3   Once the mash is cold, add the diced mozzarella, the egg yolks and the chopped parsley.

4   Divide the mixture into 24 pieces. Roll these into cylinder shapes on a lightly floured surface.

5   With the beaten eggs in one bowl and the breadcrumbs in another, coat the croquettes first in the egg, then in the crumbs. Repeat to give them a double coating.

6   Preheat the oil to 190°C/375°F and deep-fry the croquettes until golden brown, about 5-6 minutes. Drain on kitchen paper and serve straight away.

Dauphinoise in a Pan

To my mind this is still the best potato dish you can serve in winter. Yes, it's French, and purists will complain that traditionally it's cooked in layers raw in the oven, and not with the cheese. But I'm all for making life easier, and this recipe takes a quarter of the time to cook. When working in France at a three-star Michelin restaurant, this is all I was allowed to eat.

Serves 6

900g (2lb) King Edward potatoes
25g (1oz) unsalted butter
2 garlic cloves, peeled and
    chopped
2 shallots, peeled and chopped
150ml (5fl oz) milk
600ml (1 pint) double cream
salt and freshly ground black
    pepper
55g (2oz) Cheddar, grated
100g (3½oz) mozzarella,
    crumbled
salt and freshly ground black
    pepper

1   Peel and slice the potatoes as thinly as possible (preferably using a mandolin). Melt the butter in a medium heatproof dish or in a large pan, and sauté the garlic and shallot lightly. Add the milk and cream and bring to a simmer. Add the sliced potato, and cook on a gentle simmer for about 8-10 minutes to just cook the potato.

2   Preheat the grill to medium-hot.

3   Season the potatoes well, and either leave in the dish to serve or ladle carefully from the pan into 6 small heatproof dishes. Top with the cheeses, spreading them evenly. Place under the grill for a couple of minutes until brown, then serve.

PUDS

Puds are my thing! Sponge puds, fruit puds, pancakes, ice-creams... they all taste fantastic to me. Of course, we shouldn't be eating heavy puddings every day of the week. But there really can't be any harm in treating ourselves and our families every once in a while, can there? Remember how good classics like Queen of Puds tasted when we were kids? Well, they taste just as good now!

Chocolate and Marron Glacé Tart

Sugared marrons glacés and roasted fresh chestnuts are a must at Christmas. You might stuff them fresh inside your turkey, but you could try the sugared ones in this quick and simple dessert. This is one of those puds that gets a little better after a day in the fridge.

Serves 8

75ml (2½fl oz) dark rum
55g (2oz) caster sugar
200g (7oz) marrons glacés, chopped
400g (14oz) good-quality chocolate cake
375g (13oz) good dark chocolate, broken into pieces
560ml (20½fl oz) double cream
good cocoa powder
100ml (3½fl oz) pouring cream or double cream, semi-whipped

1   Heat the rum and 50ml (2fl oz) water in a pan with the sugar. When hot, remove the pan from the heat. Allow to cool, then add the chopped marrons glacés.

2   Slice the chocolate cake and use it to line the base of a 25cm (10in) flan tin. Scatter an even layer of the rum and marron glacés mixture over the top, using up all the mixture.

3   Melt the chocolate in a bowl over a pan of hot water. Allow to cool slightly before adding the cream. The mixture should go smooth and glossy. Spoon this over the surface of the marrons and cake.

4   Place the tart in the fridge to set overnight or for at least a few hours before serving.

5   Dust with cocoa powder, then serve sliced with a drizzle of pouring cream or a spoonful of the semi-whipped cream on the side.

Cranachan

I bet that no more than a few weeks after this book's out some Scot will comes up to me to say this recipe is all wrong. It's great, but then how could it not be? Cream, whisky and raspberries – it's one of the few cold desserts I know that will warm your cockles on a winter's day.

Serves 8

85g (3oz) pinhead oatmeal
3 tbsp whisky
600ml (1 pint) double cream
85g (3oz) caster sugar
450g (1lb) raspberries

1   Put the oatmeal on a baking tray and toast briefly under the grill, taking care not to burn it. Remove and, while still warm, sprinkle over the whisky and leave to stand for 10 minutes.

2   While the oatmeal is absorbing the whisky, whip the double cream, adding the caster sugar as it starts to hold, and continue to whisk until it forms soft peaks. Be careful not to take it too far, or the cream will split.

3   Fold the oatmeal into the cream and spoon the mixture into some large wine glasses.

4   Divide the raspberries between the glasses, sitting them on top of the cream. Chill for 30 minutes to firm up before serving.

Classic Lemon Posset

Simple is always the best, and this is incredibly simple! For something extra special, place some crushed biscuits and a dollop of home-made lemon curd (but it must be home-made, or the stuff you get at a WI stall in the market) in the bottom.

Serves 6

600ml (1 pint) double cream
140g (5oz) caster sugar
juice of 2 large lemons and finely
   grated zest of 4 large lemons

1   Put the double cream in a large pan and add the sugar. Bring this slowly to the boil, boil for 3 minutes, then leave to cool.

2   Add the lemon juice and half the lemon zest and whisk well until thickened. Pour into 6 large serving glasses and refrigerate for 3 hours.

3   Sprinkle with the remaining lemon zest before serving.

White Chocolate and Raspberry Trifle

This can also be made as individual trifles.

Serves 4

175g (6oz) white chocolate
2 medium egg yolks
25g (1oz) caster sugar
300ml (10fl oz) milk
700ml (1¼ pints) double cream
8 x 4cm (1½in) slices Swiss roll
   (bought or home-made)
2 tbsp kirsch
600g (1lb 5oz) raspberries
a few fresh mint sprigs

1 Put a 55g (2oz) piece of white chocolate in the fridge – this will make it easier to grate later. Break the remainder into small pieces.

2 Cream the egg yolks and caster sugar together in a large bowl. Whisk for about 2-3 minutes, until the mixture is pale, thick and creamy and leaves a trail.

3 Pour the milk and 175ml (6fl oz) of the cream into a small, heavy-based saucepan and bring to the boil. Pour this on to the egg mixture, whisking all the time, then pour it back into the pan and place over a moderate heat. Stir the mixture with a wooden spoon until it starts to thicken and coats the back of the spoon. Add the broken-up pieces of chocolate and stir in until completely incorporated. Remove the pan from the heat and allow to cool slightly. Cover the custard with clingfilm to stop a skin forming.

4 Place half the Swiss roll slices in a large glass bowl and sprinkle with half the kirsch. Scatter over a third of the raspberries, then repeat. Pour the white chocolate custard over the top and leave to set in the fridge.

5 To serve, whip the remaining double cream. Top the custard with a the whipped cream, scatter over the remaining raspberries, grate over the chilled white chocolate and place the mint sprigs on top.

Syrup Sponge with Crushed Raspberries

This sponge pudding should be made in a microwave, as it doesn't steam successfully. It'll take you no longer than 10 minutes.

Serves 4

150g (5½oz) plain flour
1 tsp baking powder
125g (4½oz) unsalted butter, melted
125g (4½oz) caster sugar
2 medium eggs
juice and finely grated zest of 2 small lemons
25ml (1fl oz) milk
vegetable oil, for greasing
4 tbsp golden syrup, or jam if preferred
100g (3½oz) raspberries (fresh if possible, but home-frozen would do)

1 Sift the flour and baking powder together into a bowl. Tip the butter, sugar, eggs, flour and baking powder into a food processor and mix to a paste. Add the lemon juice and zest and continue to mix, adding the milk, until the mixture reaches a dropping consistency.

2 Grease a 1.2-litre (40fl oz) basin suitable for the microwave with a little vegetable oil. Pour in a little of the syrup and all the raspberries. Spoon in the sponge mixture, cover with clingfilm and microwave on full power for 4 minutes (or until the sponge begins to shrink from the side and is springy to the touch).

3 Leave to stand for 2-3 minutes before turning out. Serve with the remaining syrup or jam, and with some "proper" custard if you like (*see* page 70).

Sussex Pond Pudding

This is the best dessert ever, but be warned that it takes a while to make. This is not a dish ever likely to appear at a Weight Watchers' convention dinner, as the amount of butter and sugar is frightening! But you'll forget all about that when you pour double cream over it and have a spoon in your hand…

Serves 4-6

225g (8oz) self-raising flour
115g (4oz) shredded beef suet
75ml (2½fl oz) milk
200g (7oz) slightly salted butter, diced
200g (7oz) soft light brown or caster sugar
2 large lemons

1 Mix the flour and suet together in a bowl. Combine the milk with 75ml (2½fl oz) water in a jug. Mix enough of the wet ingredients into the dry ingredients to make a dough that is soft, but not too soft to roll. Roll this dough out into a large circle, then cut out a quarter of the circle to be used later as the lid of the pudding.

2 Butter a 1.5 litre (2¾ pint) pudding basin lavishly. Drop the three-quarter circle of pastry into it and press the cut sides together to make a perfect join.

3 Put 100g (3½oz) each of the butter and sugar into the pastry-lined basin. Prick the lemons all over with a larding needle so the juices can escape, then put them on to the butter and sugar. Fill the rest of the cavity with the remaining butter and sugar, adding more if you wish to.

4 Lay the reserved pastry on top of the filling and press the edges together so the pudding is sealed in. Put a piece of foil right over the basin with a pleat in the middle. Tie it in place with string and make a string handle over the top so the pudding can be lifted out easily.

5 Put a large pan of water on to boil and lower the pudding into it. The water must be boiling, and it should come halfway, or a little further, up the sides of the basin. Cover and leave to boil for 3-4 hours. If the water gets low, replenish it with boiling water.

6 To serve, remove the basin from the pan and take off the foil lid. Put a deep dish over the basin and quickly turn the whole thing upside down. It is a good idea to ease the pudding from the sides of the basin with a knife first. Put on the table and serve immediately.

Apple Charlotte

This is a classic that never fails to impress. It has to be made with Bramley apples. If you don't want to use apples, try rhubarb or a mix of apples and rhubarb. You could make it in one large dish (when it would take 30-40 minutes to cook) or four small ones, as here. Chuck custard, double cream or ice-cream on it and dive in.

Serves 4

1 kg (2¼ lb) Bramley apples
juice of 1 lemon
175g (6oz) unsalted butter
125g (4½ oz) caster sugar
4 tbsp smooth apricot jam
10 thin slices white bread,
   crusts removed

1 Preheat the oven to 180°C/350°F/gas mark 4.

2 Peel, core and slice the apples, place them in a bowl and pour over the lemon juice.

3 In a large pan, melt 25g (1oz) of the butter, then add the sugar, apples and any lemon juice. Put the lid on and cook over a gentle heat for about 10 minutes, stirring occasionally.

4 Remove the lid and cook for a further 5-10 minutes, until you have a smooth purée. Add the apricot jam and allow to cool.

5 Meanwhile, melt the remaining butter. Cut the slices of bread in half, and then cut each half into 4 slices to get small fingers. Dip each piece of bread into the melted butter and use to line 4 small dariole moulds about 6cm (2½ in) wide. Reserve some slices, dipped in butter, for lids.

6 Once the moulds are lined, spoon in the apple purée and top with the remaining bread slices. Bake for 15 minutes, or until golden on top.

7 Remove from the oven and allow to cool slightly. Carefully turn out and serve immediately.

Queen of Puddings

How can I describe this dish? Well, it's like a custard tart and lemon meringue pie rolled into one. I remember my auntie used to make it, along with stuff like pink blancmange, jam tarts – oh, and dripping cake. They all tasted good then, and they taste even better now, as they bring back so many memories.

Serves 6-8

250ml (9fl oz) milk
250ml (9fl oz) double cream
1 vanilla pod, split
100g (3½oz) caster sugar
6 medium egg yolks
140g (5oz) fresh breadcrumbs
finely grated zest of 2 lemons
200g (7oz) raspberry jam

MERINGUE
4 medium egg whites
115g (4oz) caster sugar
1 tbsp icing sugar

1 To make the custard, pour the milk and cream into a pan and add the split vanilla pod. Bring to the boil over a medium heat.

2 In a bowl, whisk the sugar into the egg yolks until it is well dissolved and the mixture is light and creamy. Slowly pour in the hot milk and cream, whisking all the time. Remove the vanilla pod.

3 Mix in the breadcrumbs and lemon zest, then pour into an ovenproof glass or ceramic baking dish of about 20 x 25 x 5cm (8 x 10 x 2in). Allow to stand for 10-15 minutes.

4 Meanwhile, preheat the oven to 150°C/300°F/gas mark 2, and have a roasting tin ready, half-full of boiling water (a bain-marie).

5 Place the baking dish in the bain-marie in the centre of the oven and bake for 25-30 minutes, until the custard is still slightly wobbly in the centre. Remove and allow to cool.

6 Whack the oven temperature up to 190°C/375°F/gas mark 5.

7 For the meringue, whisk the egg whites until stiff, then whisk in the caster sugar – apart from 1 tbsp.

8 Melt the jam in a pan and spread it over the custard. Cover the pudding with the meringue mix, sprinkle with the remaining caster sugar and the icing sugar, and bake for 10-15 minutes, until the top is crisp and lightly browned. Serve straight away.

Risen Pancakes with Fresh Fruit and Maple Syrup

These are like crumpets, but easier and quicker to make. They will freeze well, but must be layered between sheets of greaseproof paper or else they'll all stick together. Warm them up on a tray in a low oven.

Serves 8

175g (6oz) self-raising flour
1 tbsp baking powder
100g (3½oz) caster sugar
2 medium eggs, beaten
275ml (9½fl oz) milk
unsalted butter

TO SERVE
200g (7oz) mixed fresh fruit
   (strawberries, raspberries,
   and blueberries)
100ml (3½fl oz) maple syrup

1   To make the pancakes, sift the flour into a bowl with the baking powder and caster sugar. Add the eggs and milk and whisk together, but be careful not to over-mix.

2   Heat a little butter in a non-stick pan, then add 2 tbsp of batter for each pancake. Once golden brown, turn over and cook on the other side, about 2 minutes in all. Repeat, using a little more butter, until you have used all the batter.

3   Serve the pancakes with the fresh fruit on top. Drizzle over some maple syrup.

Cheat's Raspberry and Cassis Ripple Ice-cream

When serving this, hide the ice-cream cartons to make it look like you did it all yourself. It's tastes fantastic!

Serves 8

2 litres (3½ pints) vanilla ice-cream, partly thawed in the fridge until just soft

CASSIS SAUCE
300g (10½oz) frozen raspberries
25g (1oz) caster sugar
juice and finely grated zest of ½ lemon
3 tbsp cassis

1 To make the sauce, blend the raspberries, sugar, lemon juice and zest and cassis. Pass it through a sieve to remove the raspberry seeds.

2 Drizzle the sauce over the ice-cream and quickly marble it through, using a folding motion with a spoon.

3 Place the ice-cream in a freezer-proof container and freeze it for 3-4 hours before serving.

Blood Orange Ice-cream

The custard base here could be used for other ice-creams: add a little vanilla extract for a vanilla ice or some other fruit flavourings. You could also add some brandy to this custard for a brandy sauce for Christmas pud.

Serves 6

500g (1lb 2oz) blood oranges, preferably unwaxed
350g (12oz) caster sugar
6 medium egg yolks
200ml (7fl oz) double cream
400ml (14fl oz) full-fat milk

1   Finely grate the orange zest into a bowl, then quarter the fruits. Put the quarters into the bowl as well, and pour over 250g (9oz) of the caster sugar. Refrigerate, covered, for a day or so.

2   Squeeze the juice from the mixture – start by using your hands, then press through a nylon sieve. Measure the juice and discard the pulp.

3   Make the custard for the ice-cream by whisking the egg yolks and remaining sugar together until thick and pale. This should take 10 minutes in a food mixer.

4   Bring the cream and milk to the boil in heavy-bottomed pan, then whisk this into the eggs. Return the pan to the heat and cook gently, stirring constantly, until the custard begins to thicken. Do not allow the mixture to boil or it will scramble. If you prefer, you can cook the custard in a bowl set over a pan of simmering water. Check whether it is thick enough by coating the back of a wooden spoon with it; if, when you slide your finger through it, it leaves a trail, it is ready. Remove from the heat and cool.

5   Whisk the juice with 1½ times its volume of cooled custard, then churn in an ice-cream maker. Alternatively, pour the mixture into freezer-proof containers and half-freeze, then whisk again to remove the ice crystals. Return to the freezer.

TARTS

I've had some very happy times as a pastry chef – particularly inventing (and tasting) new tarts! This chapter includes some of my favourites. Believe me, home-made pastry is incredibly easy to make and tastes a million times nicer than the shop-bought stuff. My recommendation is that you make enough pastry for two flan rings, and then bung one in the freezer – it freezes brilliantly.

Sweet Shortcrust Pastry

Making pastry may seem like hard work, but it's worth it. It's not just that the flavour and texture are better than that of the shop-bought stuff – it makes you feel good, too. It makes me think of my gran, who never overworked the dough or used too much flour (which can toughen it and make it shrink when cooking).

Lines a 23cm (9in) diameter, 3cm (1½in) deep flan ring

115g (4oz) cold unsalted butter, cubed
225g (8oz) plain white flour
a pinch of salt
2 tbsp caster sugar
2 tbsp ground almonds
1 egg, lightly beaten, plus extra to glaze

Note: It's a good idea to double the quantity to line two flan rings, so you can use one and put the other in the freezer.

1   Place the butter, flour, salt, sugar and almonds in a food processor. Blitz until you have a fine breadcrumb texture, but do not overwork. Add the egg and ½ an egg-shell full of cold water and mix well, using the pulse button until the pastry balls; again, do not overwork.

2   Turn the pastry out of the processor and knead very gently, just to bring it together. If you have doubled the mixture, divide the pastry in two. Flatten each piece of dough slightly (this makes it easier to roll when chilled) and wrap in cling-film, then chill in the fridge for at least 20 minutes – an hour or two would be better.

3   Grease your tart tin. Lightly flour the work surface. Roll the pastry out so you end up with a circle about 4cm (1½in) larger in diameter than the flan ring. Carefully roll the pastry on to the rolling pin and then unroll it over the flan ring, taking care not stretch the pastry too much.

4   Immediately ease the pastry into the ring and use your thumb to gently push it into the bottom and corners of the ring; do not leave any creases in the outside or air between the pastry and the ring. Leave about 1cm (½in) overhanging the top edge of the ring. Then trim off with a sharp knife or roll a rolling pin over the top to remove the excess. Use your thumb to squeeze up the top edge again (the pastry will shrink back a little during cooking), and pinch with your thumb and forefinger to make the edge more decorative. Using a piece of well-floured leftover pastry, push the bottom of the flan into the corners so it's nice and flush. Chill for 30 minutes. Preheat the oven to 200°C/400°F/gas mark 6.

5   Cut out a round piece of greaseproof paper 4cm (1½in) larger than the flan and place it inside the pastry-lined flan tin. Fill with baking beans and blind bake for 15 minutes, or until the top edge is slightly brown. Remove the paper and beans, turn the oven down to 160°C/325°F/gas mark 3, and cook for a further 10 minutes, until the pastry is set but has taken no colour. Remove from the oven, brush with beaten egg (to stop the pastry getting soggy when you add the filling), and then put it back in the oven for 2 minutes to seal. Cool for a little while before adding the filling.

When you first turn the pastry out of the processor, gently knead it.

Flatten the pastry slightly, wrap it, then chill it for at least 20 minutes.

Roll out the pastry on a lightly floured work surface.

You need a circle 4cm (1½ in) bigger than your tart ring.

Push the pastry into the bottom and corners of the ring.

Line the pastry case with greaseproof and pour in baking beans.

Chocolate and Raspberry Tarts with Fennel

This is on my restaurant menu. It might seem peculiar to put fennel with chocolate, but it's a mix I love. You can use fennel, aniseed or Pernod. The idea came from The French Laundry restaurant in California, where they bake chocolate almost like fondant with a fennel truffle as a soft, liquid centre. I've simplified it by making a tart with raspberries.

Serves 4

butter, for greasing
1/2 recipe sweet shortcrust pastry
   (see page 76)
plain flour, for dusting

FILLING
350g (12oz) bitter chocolate,
   broken into pieces
4 medium eggs
55g (2oz) caster sugar
75ml (2 1/2 fl oz) double cream
200g (7oz) raspberries

GARNISH
cocoa powder
vanilla ice-cream
fresh mint sprigs
fennel oil (*see* opposite)

1 Preheat the oven to 190°C/375°F/gas mark 5, and grease 8 x 7.5cm (3in) plain-edged tart tins.

2 Roll out the pastry on a lightly floured surface and use to line the tins (*see* page 76). Prick the bases with a fork and bake for about 15-20 minutes. Allow to cool and then keep in the tins.

3 For the filling, melt the chocolate carefully in a bowl over simmering water. In another bowl, whisk up the eggs and sugar, then fold in the cream and melted chocolate.

4 Spoon this mixture into the baked pastry cases and sprinkle with the raspberries. Bake for 10 more minutes, until just slightly cooked.

5 Serve warm with a dusting of cocoa powder, a scoop of ice-cream, a sprig of fresh mint and some fennel oil around the edge.

Fennel Oil

I really like this. Let's face it: we make a cake with carrots, so why not do this? Anise works well in a baked mousse I make in the restaurant. I used to make this with a stock syrup and blended fennel through it, but I find it works better with olive oil.

Makes 300ml (10fl oz)

salt
30g (1oz) fresh flat-leaf parsley leaves
1 large fennel bulb, finely chopped
300ml (10fl oz) good olive oil

1   Bring a pot of salted water to the boil. Place the parsley leaves in a strainer and dip them into the water for 10-15 seconds, keeping the water at a strong boil. Remove the strainer and plunge the blanched parsley into an ice-water bath to chill.

2   Drain the cold parsley and squeeze as dry as possible.

3   Place all the parsley and chopped fennel in a blender with enough of the oil just to cover. Turn on the blender to medium speed and blend for a minute. Turn the speed to high and continue to blend for 2 minutes.

4   Pass the finished oil through a fine sieve or a clean tea-towel. Store the oil in the refrigerator or freeze. Use as required.

Bitter Chocolate Tart

You need the best chocolate for pastries, but don't listen to chefs who tell you to use over 70 per cent cocoa solids. The max you need is 70 per cent, otherwise you can't eat the stuff. Serve this tart warm and never refrigerate it once cooked. To make it even more special, make a chocolate pastry case: substitute 35g (1¼oz) of the flour with cocoa powder.

Serves 6-8

200g (7oz) bitter chocolate, 70% cocoa solids (no more)
100g (3½oz) milk chocolate
2 large eggs, plus 2 large egg yolks, at room temperature
60g (2¼oz) caster sugar
150g (5½oz) unsalted butter, melted
1 x 23cm (9in) plain or chocolate sweet shortcrust pastry case, baked blind (see page 76)
icing sugar

COFFEE BEAN SYRUP
2 tbsp liquid glucose
10 fresh coffee beans, crushed
200g (7oz) caster sugar
juice of ½ lemon

1 Preheat the oven to 220°C/425°F/gas mark 7.

2 Break the 2 chocolates into pieces, and melt together in a heatproof bowl over a pan of gently simmering water.

3 Place the eggs, egg yolks and sugar in the bowl of a food mixer and whisk at high speed until very thick. Remove the bowl from the machine and carefully stir in the melted chocolate, taking care not to knock too much air out of the eggs. Fold in the melted butter, again very carefully.

4 Place the blind-baked flan case on a baking sheet, pour the chocolate mixture into the pastry shell, and bake for 7-8 minutes, or until just set – do not let the edges soufflé up. Remove from the oven and leave to cool on a wire rack.

5 Meanwhile, make the coffee bean syrup. Place 225ml (8fl oz) cold water, the glucose, coffee beans and sugar in a pan and bring to the boil. Remove from the heat, cover and allow to cool. Finally, add lemon juice to taste to the cooled syrup, then strain to remove the coffee beans.

6 Eat the tart at room temperature, cut into wedges, dusted heavily with icing sugar, accompanied by the coffee syrup.

Quick Chocolate Tart

As you can see by the number of chocolate tarts I've included in this book, it's one of my favourite things to eat! This one is quite quick to prepare, but looks and tastes no less special because of that.

Serves 12

PASTRY
255g (9oz) unsalted butter, softened
40g (1½oz) icing sugar
1 medium egg
500g (1lb 2oz) plain flour, sifted

CHOCOLATE FILLING
350ml (12fl oz) double cream
140ml (¼ pint) full fat milk
400g (14oz) dark chocolate (at least 70% cocoa solids), broken into pieces
3 medium eggs, beaten

1 Preheat the oven to 180°C/350°F/gas mark 4. Place a baking sheet on the middle shelf in the oven.

2 Cream the butter and sugar in a food mixer, or in a bowl with a wooden spoon, until pale and fluffy, then add the egg.

3 Turn the food mixer to its lowest setting and add the plain flour. Mix until the pastry comes together. Wrap in cling-film and chill for at least 30 minutes.

4 Butter a 20cm (8in) tart ring or loose-bottomed tart tin. Roll out the pastry into a circle 3mm (⅛in) thick and about 5cm (2in) bigger than the tart ring. Line the tart ring with the pastry, pressing it down gently and leaving a 2.5cm (1in) overhang.

5 Prick the base with a fork and blind bake for 20 minutes, or until starting to brown. Remove and trim the overhanging pastry level with the top of the ring, using a sharp, heavy knife.

6 Turn the oven down to 130°C/250°F/gas mark ½. To make the filling, in a saucepan heat the cream and milk until trembling, just under boiling point. Take off the heat. Add the chocolate to the cream and milk and stir until fully blended, then add the beaten eggs and mix again.

7 Pour the chocolate mixture into the tart case and bake for about 1 hour. The tart is done when it is still a bit wobbly in the middle. Leave to set for at least 45 minutes before serving. Serve with the orange ice-cream on page 73.

Pecan Pie

I find this quite hard to cook, as it appears to be cooked long before it is. If you're unsure, turn the oven a bit lower and cook for a while longer or else the nuts will burn.

Serves 8

350g (12oz) pecans (or walnuts)
55g (2oz) bitter chocolate, grated
1 tsp vanilla extract
2 pinches salt
350ml (12fl oz) good maple syrup
4 large eggs
300g (10½oz) granulated sugar
115g (4oz) unsalted butter, melted
1 x 23cm (9in) sweet shortcrust
    pastry case, baked blind (*see*
    page 76)

1 Preheat the oven to 170°C/325°F/gas mark 3.

2 Place the nuts, grated chocolate, vanilla extract, salt and maple syrup in a bowl. Beat the eggs in a separate bowl, then stir into the nut mixture together with the sugar. Finally add the melted butter and stir well.

3 Pour into the prepared pastry case and bake for 55-60 minutes, or until set in the middle. Allow to cool completely before cutting.

Plum and Almond Tart

This is a twist on a prune and almond tart, but it works better, as the plums stew down while the tart is cooking. Use dark plums to give the frangipane a rich colour once cooked. Fluff the butter and sugar for the frangipine together well before adding the eggs and flour, as this will create a much lighter filling – and never put the cooked tart in the fridge.

Serves 8

butter, for greasing
400g (14oz) sweet shortcrust
   pastry (*see* page 76)
plain flour, for dusting
900g (2lb) plums, dark if you can
   get them
icing sugar

FRANGIPANE
225g (8oz) unsalted butter
225g (8oz) caster sugar
4 eggs, beaten
4 tbsp brandy
115g (4oz) ground almonds
4 tbsp plain flour

TO SERVE
100ml (3½fl oz) double cream
   plus cassis to taste (optional) or
   4 tbsp ready-made custard
   (bought or home-made, *see*
   page 70)
a few blackberries (optional)

1 Preheat the oven to 200°C/400°F/gas mark 6.

2 Grease and line a 34cm (13½in) round fluted or rectangular tart tin. Roll out the pastry on a lightly floured surface, press it into the tin, trim the edges and prick the base lightly with a fork. Cover and chill.

3 Meanwhile, make the frangipane. Using an electric whisk, beat together the butter and sugar until pale and creamy. Gradually beat in the eggs. Stir in the brandy, almonds and flour. Spread the frangipane evenly over the case of the pastry case.

4 Remove the stones from the plums and cut into quarters. Gently push the plum quarters vertically into the frangipane.

5 Place the tart on a baking sheet and bake for 10-15 minutes, or until the pastry is beginning to brown. Reduce the oven temperature to 180°C/350°F/gas mark 4 and continue to bake for 35 minutes.

6 Remove the tart from the oven and leave to cool slightly, then remove from the tin and dust lightly with icing sugar.

7 Serve the tart at room temperature. Cut it into wedges and serve it warm with plain, thick double cream, double cream flavoured with cassis, or custard, and perhaps a few blackberries.

Bramley Apple, Custard and Honey Tart

This is a great dish! Roughly puréed Bramleys (the king of British apples) form the base, and are topped with slices of Cox's. Custard is poured on the top, but don't rush cooking the custard, as you'll risk it "souffléing" and so splitting on the surface. If you are unsure, cook the tart for a bit longer and pop it in the fridge to firm the custard before you serve it.

Serves 4-6

1 x 23cm (9in) sweet shortcrust pastry case, baked blind (*see* page 76)

FILLING
2 large Bramley apples
caster sugar
1 large Cox's apple
20g (³/₄oz) unsalted butter
4 medium egg yolks
2 medium eggs
2 tbsp clear honey
700ml (1¼ pints) double cream
a pinch of saffron strands (optional)

TO SERVE (OPTIONAL)
1 large Cox's apple
icing sugar
a little whipped cream

1 Preheat the oven to 170°C/325°F/gas mark 3.

2 Peel, core and roughly slice the Bramleys. Put them in a pan with a little water, and cook over a medium heat for 5-10 minutes, until soft. Add some sugar to taste and beat to a purée.

3 Peel and core the Cox's apple, and cut it into neat 5mm (¹/₄in) slices. Fry gently in the unsalted butter until softened and lightly coloured. Place the apple purée in the bottom of the pastry case and overlap the apple slices on top.

4 In a bowl, beat together the egg yolks, eggs and honey. Place the cream and saffron (if using) in a small pan and bring to the boil. When boiling, whisk the cream into the egg mix, beating all the time. Pour into the pastry case, over the apple, and bake for 20 minutes, until the mixture has set and is golden brown.

5 If you want to garnish with caramelized apple, peel and core the Cox's apple and cut it into slices, 3cm (1¹/₄in) thick. Sprinkle with icing sugar and toast under a hot grill until caramelized. Serve the tart warm or at room temperature with a few pieces of caramelized apple and a dollop of cream on each slice.

HALLOWE'EN AND BONFIRE NIGHT

I have so many brilliant memories of Hallowe'en and Bonfire Night when I was a kid – running down the hill to see the fireworks and get one of granny's baked potatoes, scoffing my auntie's toffee from a waxed bag, and cooking marshmallows on the bonfire. Nothing could beat it!

Spicy Bean Stew with Sausages

Most adults and kids love this because it's so simple to make. Onions and garlic are used as a base, and good-quality sausages are the key. Cut them up into pieces, fry them all, add some canned beans and tomatoes, and stew down for about 15 minutes. Beautiful! I served this at a truckers' café once, but for breakfast, and 150 of them woofed it down!

Serves 4

5 tbsp olive or vegetable oil
8 good free-range pork sausages
4 streaky bacon rashers, chopped
1 medium onion, peeled and
   chopped
2 garlic cloves, peeled and
   chopped
1 red chilli, chopped (or more if it
   is really cold!)
1 tbsp soft brown sugar
2 x 400g cans plum or chopped
   tomatoes
a dash of red/white wine
   (whatever is open)
2 x 300g cans cannellini beans,
   drained and rinsed
1 x 300g can kidney beans,
   drained and rinsed
leaves from small bunch of fresh
   parsley, chopped
salt and freshly ground black
   pepper

1 Place a large heavy-based saucepan on the hob and heat 3 tbsp of the oil. Add the sausages and fry over a medium heat, turning them over until they are browned on the outside. Take them out of the pan and chop them into 4cm (1½in) pieces. Set them aside on a plate.

2 Add the remaining oil to the pan, turn the heat down to low, add the bacon and onion, and fry gently for around 10 minutes, stirring from time to time so that they don't catch on the bottom. They will pick up all the lovely sausagey goo in the bottom of the pan.

3 Add the garlic and chilli and fry for another couple of minutes, then add the brown sugar. Pour in the tomatoes, wine and 300ml (10fl oz) water, then stir in the sausage pieces along with the beans, and cook for 15-20 minutes over a low-medium heat.

4 Stir in the chopped parsley, salt and lots of black pepper, and serve with some nice fresh crusty bread or mashed potato.

Salt-baked Baby Potatoes with Taleggio and Bacon

I loved baby jacket potatoes at Hallowe'en or Bonfire Night as a kid. I remember rushing to the bottom of the hill to see the fireworks and to dive into my granny's baked potatoes with bacon and Stilton (and to scoff the last toffee apples). There are many cheeses available now – you could use dolcelatte torta or my favourite, which is taleggio.

Serves 6-8

140g (5oz) Maldon sea salt
16-20 baby roasting potatoes
140g (5oz) taleggio cheese
4 streaky bacon rashers, chopped
    and blanched in boiling water

1 Preheat the oven to 230°C/450°F/gas mark 8.

2 Cover a baking tray with a layer of sea salt flakes. Lay the potatoes on the salt and bake for 30-40 minutes, or until cooked through.

3 Cut a slit in the top of each potato and stuff with the cheese and blanched bacon.

4 Place the stuffed potatoes back in the oven or put under a well preheated grill for a few minutes, until the cheese has melted and the bacon is cooked through and golden.

5 Serve immediately, while still hot.

Classic Beef Burgers with Soft Onions

I remember some top chefs and I discussing which dish had changed the way we ate over the past 10 years, and we all agreed it was the humble burger! Make them with quality mince so you can serve them nice and pink. Prepare them in advance so they can firm up in the fridge before frying. If you're going to barbecue them, seal them in a pan first.

Serves 4

900g (2lb) best minced beef
salt and ground black pepper
3 white onions, peeled and thinly
    sliced
30g (1¼oz) unsalted butter
olive oil

TO SERVE
4 burger buns
1 head little gem lettuce, separated
2 medium tomatoes, sliced

1   Place the meat in a bowl and season. Weigh the meat into 225g (8oz) portions and mould them with your hands into burger shapes. Place the burgers on a tray or plate, cover with clingfilm and leave in the fridge.

2   When you want to eat the burgers, sauté the onions in a pan in the butter until golden brown, about 10-15 minutes.

3   Heat a little olive oil in a ridged cast-iron griddle or sauté pan and fry the burgers, depending how you like them. You need 3 minutes each side for medium. Serve the burgers in the buns with a couple of lettuce leaves, some sliced tomato and some soft onion.

Home-made Tomato Ketchup

This pays homage to the 16 tomato plants I have in my greenhouse. I sold a few bottles of this at farmers' markets this year, but I'm not selling them any more – they're too good!

Makes 600ml (1 pint)

1 clove
1 bay leaf
a few coriander seeds
½ cinnamon stick (optional)
250ml (9fl oz) cider vinegar
8 tbsp demerara or caster sugar
1.5kg (3lb 5oz) quartered and
    seeded ripe tomatoes
1 tsp salt
1 tsp English mustard powder
1 garlic clove, peeled and crushed
a dash of Tabasco sauce
1 tbsp tomato purée

1   Tie the clove, bay, coriander and cinnamon stick, if using, in a piece of muslin. Place the vinegar and sugar in a heavy-based pan and bring to a simmer. Add the tomatoes and all the other ingredients, including the muslin bag, and bring to the boil, stirring to prevent any sticking. Once up to the boil, reduce the temperature and simmer, stirring occasionally, for 40 minutes. Be careful the mix doesn't stick to the base of the pan.

2   Discard the muslin bag, blitz the ketchup in a food processor or liquidizer, and push through a sieve. Store in sterilized bottles, seal, and keep in a cool place for 3-4 weeks for before using. If you find the ketchup to be loose and thin once cold, simply re-boil and thicken with a little cornflour or arrowroot mixed to a paste with water.

Roast Squash, Lemon and Mustard Purée

This is a good dish to serve with roast meat, poultry or game, and makes a nice change from mashed spuds every time.

Serves 6-8

2 butternut squashes, about 650g (1lb 7oz) each
2 garlic cloves, peeled and crushed
2 lemons, each cut into 4 slices
1 tbsp olive oil
1 sprig fresh thyme, leaves picked off
90g (3¼oz) unsalted butter
3 tbsp coarse-grain mustard
5 tbsp double cream
salt and freshly ground black pepper

1 Preheat the oven to 190°C/375°F/gas mark 5.

2 Cut the squashes in half, scoop out the seeds, then peel and chop the flesh into even-sized chunks. Place the squash in a bowl with the garlic, lemons, oil and thyme.

3 Melt 55g (2oz) of the butter and add half of this to the bowl. Toss together, then spread out in a roasting tin and roast for about 20 minutes, until the squash feels tender when pierced with a knife.

4 Scoop the squash into a food processor with the remaining melted butter, the mustard, cream and seasoning. Whiz to a smooth purée. Alternatively, mash the squash and stir in the other ingredients.

5 Reheat and dot with the remaining butter when ready to serve.

Butternut Squash and Lime Soup with Pine Nuts and Herb Oil

For the first time this year I have tried to grow squash in the garden and have been amazed by all the different kinds available. The one we are most familiar with must be the common butternut, and since growing these I've become an even bigger fan. This soup is different to the norm: I roast the squash first as I think it tastes much better.

Serves 6-8

1 butternut squash, about 1kg (2¼lb)
2 tbsp clear honey
extra virgin olive oil
1 white onion, peeled and chopped
2 garlic cloves, peeled and chopped
150ml (5fl oz) white wine
500ml (18fl oz) chicken stock
25g (1oz) pine nuts
salt and freshly ground black pepper
150ml (5fl oz) double cream
finely grated zest and juice of 3 limes
50ml (2fl oz) crème fraîche
10g (¼oz) fresh basil

HERB OIL

10g (¼oz) fresh basil
20g (¾oz) fresh chervil
75ml (2½fl oz) olive oil

1 Preheat the oven to 200°C/400°F/gas mark 6.

2 Cut the squash in half, scoop out the seeds, then peel it and dice the flesh into 2.5cm (1in) chunks. Place in a large oven tray with the honey and a little olive oil. Roast for 30-40 minutes.

3 Meanwhile, fry the onion and garlic in a little olive oil to soften, then add the wine and stock. Bring to the boil and simmer for 3-4 minutes.

4 Sauté the pine nuts in a little olive oil until golden brown. Remove and leave to one side.

5 To make the herb oil, chop the basil and chervil and place in a blender with the olive oil. Blend to a fine purée. Season and leave to one side.

6 Remove the squash from the oven and place it in a blender with the stock mixture, cream, lime juice and lime zest, and blend. Season well. Return to the pan to the heat and check the seasoning.

7 Pour into individual bowls, and top with a dollop of crème fraîche. Drizzle with the puréed herb oil, pine nuts and the basil. Serve.

Puff Pastry Crusted Pumpkin and Rosemary Soup

I thought this dish up in Prince Charles' Duchy Estate in Cornwall, where I stumbled across a farm shop while filming for the BBC. It had over 30 different types of squashes! I bought a pumpkin, which I roasted when I got home and made into a great, inexpensive, vegetable soup.

Serves 6

1 small pumpkin, about 1kg (2¼lb), peeled, seeded and diced into 2.5cm (1in) chunks
1 white onion, peeled and chopped
2 garlic cloves, peeled and chopped
2 tbsp clear honey
3 fresh rosemary sprigs
extra virgin olive oil
500ml (18fl oz) fresh chicken stock
100ml (3½fl oz) white wine
150ml (5fl oz) double cream
juice of 1 lemon
salt and freshly ground black pepper

TOPPING
200g (7oz) ready-rolled puff pastry
1 egg yolk, beaten

1 Preheat the oven to 200°C/400°F/gas mark 6.

2 Place the pumpkin, onion and garlic in a large oven tray with the honey, rosemary sprigs and a little olive oil. Roast for 25-30 minutes, until the pumpkin is cooked and golden brown. Keep basting the pumpkin as the honey may catch on the bottom of the tray. Remove from the oven.

3 Heat the stock and wine on the stove. Place into a blender with the pumpkin mixture, cream and lemon juice, and blend until smooth. Check the seasoning, and keep to one side.

4 On a slightly floured work top, open out the ready-rolled pastry and, either using 4 large ovenproof soup dishes or 4 smaller deep dishes, cut the pastry out into 4 circles, 2cm (¾in) bigger than the rim of each dish.

6 Fill the dishes no more than three-quarters full with soup and brush the edges of the dishes with the beaten egg yolk. Place the pastry on top and crimp it down on to the egg to seal. Use any of the leftovers to make a small pumpkin-shaped piece on the top.

7 Brush the tops with the egg and bake for 15 minutes, until golden brown on the top. Serve piping hot.

Treacle Toffee

My auntie used to make toffee, which she served in a waxed bag, for Bonfire Night. This was really popular with all the kids! I think she learnt the recipe from my great-great-grandmother, who had a corner shop selling toffee and fudge. My auntie would make a variety of toffees – some with raisins or sultanas, some plain, some with syrup and some, of course, with black treacle. To break it up, she used an old toffee hammer that she got from Terry's Chocolates, when my father was manager of their restaurant in York (now sadly shut down). She always made it nice and soft, probably because she never fridged it. The toffee was kept in the biscuit tin with the commemorative plaque of Queen Elizabeth from when she got married, a tin which I treasure to this day. My auntie sadly passed away about 15 years ago, but the legacy of her toffee remains.

Makes about 800g (1³⁄₄lb)

450g (1lb) demerara sugar
85g (3oz) unsalted butter, softened
¹⁄₂ tsp cream of tartar
100g (3¹⁄₂oz) black treacle
100g (3¹⁄₂oz) golden syrup
a handful of sultanas

1 Place the sugar in a heavy-bottomed saucepan with 150ml (5fl oz) water and heat until all the sugar has dissolved. Add the rest of the ingredients, apart from the sultanas, and put in a sugar thermometer.

2 Bring to the boil, brushing the sides of the pan down with a pastry brush dipped in water to stop crystals forming. Do not stir. When the sugar reaches 132°C/270°F, quickly and carefully fold in the sultanas. Pour the mixture into a greaseproof-paper-lined 18cm (7in) tin and allow to cool. When set, break into pieces and store in a jar.

Toffee Apples

The first secret of good toffee apples is to get a nice apple. Make sure the apples are dry, or else the caramel won't stick. It's also important to add enough butter to your caramel.

Makes 4

8 small, dry eating apples
toffee (as above, but replacing the treacle with another 100g/3¹⁄₂oz golden syrup, increasing the butter to 115g/4oz and omitting the sultanas)

1 Make the toffee as above. When you reach the sultana stage (omitting the sultanas), stick a fork in each apple (forks are much better than sticks) and dip it into the caramel.

2 Immediately put the apple on a lightly oiled work surface or non-stick tray. Repeat with all the apples. Leave until cool and the toffee has set.

Marshmallows

Why do people buy marshmallows when they are simple to make – just a sort of royal icing with gelatine in it? The sugar must be at the right temperature before you add it to the whipped egg whites. What a fantastic way of finishing a Hallowe'en or Bonfire Night party: having a pile of these with some sticks or skewers so that you can toast them on the bonfire.

Makes 675g (1½lb)

675g (1½lb) granulated sugar
1½ tbsp liquid glucose
14 gelatine leaves
3 medium egg whites
vegetable oil
icing sugar
cornflour
1½ tsp vanilla extract

1 Put the sugar, glucose and 200ml (7fl oz) water in a heavy-based saucepan. Add a sugar thermometer. Bring to the boil and cook until it reaches 127°C/260°F.

2 Meanwhile, soak the gelatine in 150ml (5fl oz) cold water and beat the egg whites until stiff. Lightly oil a shallow baking tray, about 30 x 20cm (12 x 8in). Dust it with sieved icing sugar and cornflour.

3 When the syrup is up to temperature, carefully slide in the softened gelatine sheets and their soaking water. The syrup will bubble up, so take care not to burn yourself. Pour the syrup into a metal jug.

4 Continue to beat the egg whites – preferably with an electric whisk – while pouring in the hot syrup from the jug. Do this very slowly, or the heat will cook the egg whites too much. The mixture will become shiny and start to thicken. Add the vanilla extract and continue whisking for about 5-10 minutes, until the mixture is stiff and thick enough to hold its shape on the whisk.

5 Spoon the mixture into the prepared baking tray, and smooth it with a wet palette knife if necessary. Leave for at least an hour to set.

6 Dust the work surface with more icing sugar and cornflour. Loosen the marshmallow around the sides of the tray with a palette knife, then turn it out on to the dusted surface. Cut into squares and roll in the sugar and cornflour. Leave to dry a little on a wire rack, then pack into an airtight box or jar.

CHRISTMAS BAKING

Don't you just love Christmas baking? All those fantastic smells of dried fruit and booze – and a really good excuse to have a sneaky drink while you work! I recommend making everything yourself, including the marzipan for your Christmas cake. Go on, you'll be glad you tried it!

Christmas Cake

There are many recipes for classic Christmas cake. This is my auntie's old recipe, which worked for her, so it's good enough for me!

Makes 1 x 20cm (8in) cake

675g (1½lb) mixed dried fruit
115g (4oz) blanched flaked almonds
115g (4oz) mixed candied peel, chopped
115g (4oz) glacé cherries, well rinsed, then quartered
300g (10½oz) plain flour
1 tsp powdered cinnamon
1 tsp freshly grated nutmeg
finely grated zest and juice of 1 lemon
225g (8oz) lightly salted butter
225g (8oz) soft brown sugar, light or dark
1 tsp vanilla extract
1 tbsp black treacle
4 medium eggs
½ tsp bicarbonate of soda
1 tbsp milk
brandy

1   Preheat the oven to 140°C/275°F/gas mark 1, and line a 20cm (8in) cake tin with a layer of brown paper, then a layer of Bakewell paper.

2   Mix the dried fruit, almonds, peel and cherries in a huge bowl. Turn them well and add the flour, spices and lemon zest and juice.

3   Cream the butter and sugar thoroughly, then add the vanilla extract and treacle. Still beating, incorporate the eggs, then stir the mixture into the fruit and flour. Finally, dissolve the bicarbonate of soda in the milk and stir this into the fruit thoroughly as well. Add brandy to taste by the spoonful, until you have a soft dropping consistency.

4   Pour the mixture into the prepared tin and hollow out the top slightly. Bake for 3½ hours, then test it with a larding needle or skewer (if this is just dry, the cake is ready). Remove the cake from the oven, when it is done, and leave it to cool in its tin.

5   When cool, peel off the Bakewell and brown paper. Wrap in clingfilm, and then put into an airtight tin (or in foil). The usual thing is to keep the cake for at least a month before icing it, and to sprinkle it occasionally with more brandy.

6   To finish off the cake for Christmas, you will need marzipan and icing (*see* the recipes overleaf). Do not buy the marzipan ready-made – your own may not look as yellow as it does in the shop, but it will taste much better, I promise!

Marzipan (Almond Paste)

For some reason people still buy ready-made marzipan, particularly the fluorescent yellow stuff, which they then put on the Christmas cake they've spent ages making. Why, when marzipan can so easily be made at home?

Covers a 20cm (8in) cake

225g (8oz) icing sugar, plus extra
    for dusting
500g (1lb 2oz) ground almonds
1 large egg (weighing about
    75g/2¾oz)
3-4 tsp lemon juice

GLAZE
1 tbsp apricot jam

1 Sift the sugar into a bowl and mix in the almonds. Beat the egg well, then add it and the lemon juice to the dry ingredients. Using a wooden spoon, beat to a firm paste, then knead on a work surface that has been sprinkled with icing sugar. (If you don't find most marzipan too sweet, add another 225g/8oz sugar and use 2 medium eggs instead of 1 large.)

2 Slice the top from the cake to make it even, then turn it upside down and put it on a wire rack. Boil the jam and 1 tbsp water in a small pan, sieve it into a bowl and, while it is hot, brush some over the top (what was the bottom) of the cake.

3 Set aside a third of the marzipan and roll out the rest to a circle a little larger than the cake – do this on a sheet of clean greaseproof and use the cake tin as a guide. Press the glazed side of the cake down on to the marzipan. Remove the paper and smooth the marzipan over the sides.

4 Measure the depth of the cake and its circumference. Roll out the remaining marzipan to these measurements, again on a sheet of greaseproof. Brush the cake sides with the remaining hot apricot glaze and roll it slowly along the strip of marzipan. Pat everything into place, closing the cracks, and put the cake back on its rack.

Royal Icing

Covers a 20cm (8in) cake

4 small egg whites
4 tsp lemon juice
1kg (2 ¼ lb) icing sugar, sifted

1 Whisk the egg whites until they are white and foamy but not stiff. Stir in the lemon juice, then the sugar, bit by bit, using a wooden spoon. When everything is combined, continue to beat the mixture until it is a dazzling white. Cover the basin and leave for an hour before using.

2 To ice the cake, have a bowl of hot water handy. Put half the icing on the cake, dip the palette knife into the hot water (it shouldn't be too wet), then use it to spread the icing. Cover the cake, then put on the remaining icing, either roughly to make a snowy effect or with the aid of a forcing bag and nozzles. Leave for at least 2 days to set before eating.

Roll out the marzipan – it is easier to do this on greaseproof paper.

Brush the cake with glaze, then place the marzipan on top.

Either pat the sides down or roll a separate piece for the sides.

Use a palette knife to get a rough, snowy effect with the icing.

Stollen

I know what people are going to think of a German recipe in a British cookbook. But Stollen seems to have taken over in many shops, probably because it's a great cake. A German Christmas tradition, it's a sweet yeast bread packed with raisins, currants, citrus and cherries with a ribbon of marzipan lurking invitingly in the middle.

Serves 6-8

500g (1lb 2oz) plain white flour, sifted
½ tsp salt
125g (4½oz) unsalted butter, softened
1 tbsp baking powder
200g (7oz) unrefined caster sugar
a few drops of vanilla extract
50ml (2fl oz) dark rum
finely grated zest of 1 large lemon
1 tbsp ground mixed spice
50g (1¾oz) suet
125g (4½oz) currants
125g (4½oz) raisins
125g (4½oz) flaked almonds
40g (1½oz) chopped mixed candied peel
250g (9oz) thick crème fraîche
2 large eggs, beaten
250g (9oz) marzipan (*see* page 108)

TO FINISH
25g (1oz) melted butter
icing sugar, sifted

1 Preheat the oven to 180°C/350°F/gas mark 4. Grease a baking sheet.

2 Place the flour, salt and butter in a bowl and rub together carefully. Add the baking powder, sugar, vanilla, rum, lemon zest, mixed spice, suet, dried fruits, almonds and peel and mix well. Add the crème fraîche and beaten eggs and mix well to form a nice firm dough.

3 Place on a floured surface and gently roll out with a rolling pin to form an oblong about 30 x 46cm (12 x 18in), leaving the dough about 2cm (¾in) thick. Form the marzipan into a sausage shape the length of the dough and place it down the middle. Fold the top of the dough over the marzipan and seal well, then fold under the ends.

4 Place on the baking sheet, seam-side down, and bake for about 35-40 minutes, or until well-risen and golden brown. The cake will spread slightly, but don't worry.

5 Once cooked, remove from the oven and place on a wire rack with a piece of foil underneath. Brush liberally with melted butter and dust with plenty of icing sugar, then allow to cool.

6 Wrap tightly in foil to store; it will keep for 2-3 weeks in a cool place. Cut into large slices to serve.

Make a sausage shape of marzipan.

Put the marzipan in the middle of the dough.

Fold the dough over the marzipan.

Real Christmas Bread

There are many variations of Christmas breads, from country to country. This is my version, and it was invented purely because so often at Christmas we find we've quite a lot of mincemeat left over. It's very simple to make and uses few ingredients. I use fresh yeast, but if you can't find it, use dried (read the instructions on the packet).

Makes 1 loaf

500g (1lb 2oz) strong white flour, plus extra for dusting
100g (3½oz) mincemeat (bought or home-made, *see* page 116)
finely grated zest and juice of 2 oranges
finely grated zest and juice of 2 lemons
55g (2oz) unsalted butter
10g (¼oz) salt
25g (1oz) fresh yeast
280ml (9½fl oz) warm water

1　Place the flour, mincemeat, citrus zest and juice, butter, salt and yeast in a large bowl and mix together. Gradually mix in the warm water to form a dough.

2　Place the dough on a lightly floured surface and knead for 4 minutes. Shape into a rough sausage shape, around 15cm (6in) across. Place on a baking sheet lined with baking parchment and leave aside to rise for 1 hour, covered with a tea-towel.

3　Preheat the oven to 220°C/425°F/gas mark 7.

4　Slash the top of the loaf with a knife and dust with flour. Bake for 25 minutes, until golden brown and hollow when tapped. Cool on a wire rack.

Gran's Madeira Cake

My auntie used to make this simple and classic cake at least three times a week. Not only was it my grandad's favourite cake (the recipe came from my gran) but my uncles and I would dive into the tin at least once a day. There was never much left for my sister, only the crumbs at the bottom!

Makes 1 x 20cm (8in) cake

175g (6oz) unsalted butter, diced, plus extra for greasing
225g (8oz) self-raising flour, plus extra for dusting
175g (6oz) caster sugar
3 large eggs
30g (1¼oz) ground almonds
juice and finely grated zest of 1 lemon
2 tbsp milk

1 Preheat the oven to 180°C/350°F/gas mark 4. Use some extra butter and flour to grease and dust a 20cm (8in) square tin (or line with greaseproof). You could also use 2 x 450g (1lb) loaf tins.

2 Place the butter in the bowl of a food processor with the sugar, and blend to a light-coloured cream, scraping down the sides when needed. While the machine is running, add the eggs one by one, being careful not to split the mixture. If this happens, add a little of the flour to bring it together, but try not to get it to that stage as this will tighten up the mixture and make your cake less light and airy.

3 Add the almonds, flour, lemon juice and zest, and milk and blend quickly for 10 seconds on maximum to a smooth batter.

4 Pour the mixture into the prepared tin and bake in the bottom of the oven for 60-70 minutes (the smaller cakes for 40-45 minutes).

5 Leave to cool before storing in an airtight tin. However, if it comes out like my auntie's cakes used to, it won't be in there for long.

Yule Log

Everybody loves yule log for Christmas, which must be something to do with the amount of chocolate that goes into it. For me, it's a bit sickly, but for all you chocolate-lovers, it has to go into the book!

Serves 8

sunflower oil, for greasing
175g (6oz) plain chocolate, broken
   into pieces
6 medium eggs, separated
175g (6oz) caster sugar

FILLING

85g (3oz) plain chocolate, broken
   into pieces
200ml (7fl oz) double cream,
   whipped until thick

COATING

100g (3½oz) good plain
   chocolate, chopped
200ml (7fl oz) double cream
cocoa powder
icing sugar

1 Preheat the oven to 180°C/350°F/gas mark 4. Lightly grease a 30 x 20cm (12 x 8in) shallow Swiss roll tin with sunflower oil and line with baking parchment.

2 Put the chocolate into a small heatproof bowl over a pan of hot water and heat gently, stirring occasionally, to melt. Leave to cool.

3 Whisk the egg yolks and sugar together in a large bowl until light and creamy. Place the bowl over a pan of hot water, add the cooled chocolate and stir to blend evenly.

4 In a separate bowl, whisk the egg whites until stiff but not dry. Carefully fold into the chocolate mixture.

5 Turn the chocolate mixture into the prepared tin, tilting it so that the mixture spreads evenly into the corners. Bake for 20 minutes, or until firm to the touch.

6 Remove from the oven. Place a clean, dry tea-towel on the cake, and on top of this layer another tea-towel that has been soaked in cold water and well wrung out.

7 For the filling, melt the chocolate as above. Cool.

8 Remove the tea-towels from the sponge and turn it out on to a piece of baking parchment. Peel the lining paper from the cake. Spread the melted chocolate over the cake, then spread the whipped cream evenly on top. Roll up the cake from the long edge, using the paper to lift and help roll it forward.

9 For the coating, melt the chocolate as above. Allow it to cool slightly before adding the cream. The mixture should go smooth and glossy. Roughly spread this over the Swiss roll, then dust with cocoa powder and icing sugar. Serve.

Traditional Mincemeat

I know you're going to look at this recipe with horror because of the raw mince I've used in it. But this is the traditional way of making mincemeat. Most bought mincemeat doesn't have meat in it, of course, but I thought it would be interesting to explore. You can easily omit the steak if you want to.

Makes loads

225g (8oz) seedless raisins
350g (12oz) currants
175g (6oz) good lean rump steak,
  minced
350g (12oz) beef suet, chopped
225g (8oz) dark brown sugar
15g ($\frac{1}{2}$oz) candied citron peel,
  chopped
15g ($\frac{1}{2}$oz) candied lemon peel,
  chopped
15g ($\frac{1}{2}$oz) candied orange peel,
  chopped
$\frac{1}{4}$ small nutmeg, grated
finely grated zest and juice of
  $\frac{1}{2}$ lemon
350g (12oz) apples, weighed
  after peeling and coring,
  finely chopped
75ml (2$\frac{1}{2}$fl oz) brandy

1   Mix all the ingredients together in the order given, pouring in the brandy when everything else is well mixed together.

2   Press closely into sterilized jars to exclude the air. Cover and leave for at least a fortnight.

CHRISTMAS DAY

Christmas Day was magical when we were kids, wasn't it? The smell of spices and of the bird cooking, the twinkling lights, the presents hidden all over the house. Now I'm grown up, the excitement of Christmas is in recreating that magic for friends and their kids – in particular by cooking some delicious classic Christmas food!

Countdown to Christmas

Christmas is one of my favourite times of the year. I remember getting so excited when I was a young lad: the house was full of spicy smells; a fragrant tree hung with apples; Christmas lights and home-made biscuits dominated the sitting room; mysterious, brightly coloured parcels appeared in every corner; and then there was the ritual of hanging my stocking on the fireplace and leaving a mince pie and glass of brandy for Santa Claus.

Nowadays, the excitement is still there, but it has changed direction a little. Now I look forward to cooking up a storm, to being surrounded by family and friends, and to eating and drinking – both of which I probably do far too much!

However much we look forward to the festive season, quite a few of us combine the excitement with a sense of dread, because it always seems to involve so much buying, cooking and preparation. It's become almost like cooking for a siege. Your Christmas holiday may last only three or so days, or it may stretch to over a week. Either way, it can be a little difficult, particularly if you have a lot of people to cater for. It all comes down to good planning. The first thing to do is make a list, and you should do this some months in advance if you feel like it, because there are several elements of the traditional Christmas that can be planned and made well ahead.

Two months in advance

The sweet centrepieces of Christmas eating are the Christmas pudding, the cake and mincemeat, and all of these can be prepared well in advance of the big day.

The traditional time for making the pudding is Stir-up Sunday, around the 30 November, although I have made some as early as August. The cake can be made six weeks or so in advance, but remember to moisten it at some point with more alcohol. Both will survive well so long as they are well wrapped and kept in a cool place.

The mincemeat can be made up to two months in advance. Any other preserves will taste even better if made early and allowed a good time to mature: you will need the savoury ones for accompanying the inevitable leftover cold meats, the sweet ones for Christmas breakfasts and teas.

Think, too, about less obvious things that could be frozen for use at Christmas: stocks (good for soups, gravies and sauces), soups (always handy for a lunch or late-night snack) and ice-creams. You can freeze home-made or bought pastry for the mince pies and any canapés you might want. Basics such as butter, milk (in plastic bottles), sausage-meat and sausages can also be bought and frozen.

One month in advance

This is when you have to work your hardest. Now is the time to check your basic supplies. Have you enough flour and sugar? Is the flour past its sell-by date? How long have your powdered spices been sitting there? Buy new if necessary, for spices and flour can deteriorate over time. Have you got enough risotto rice (for a lunchtime risotto, one of the handiest recipes for times like this), basmati or other rice to go with the turkey curry? You will have plenty of leftovers, so you need basics to use with them. If you have particular baking in mind, buy foods like pistachios, dried apricots, prunes and pine nuts.

Ordering is the order of the day

Make your list for your butcher – turkey or goose, ham, sausages, bacon, eggs, sausage-meat, etc. You can collect these a day or two before Christmas, and ordering well in advance gives him plenty of time to organize himself. I would always go for a free-range turkey.

Give a list of your needs to the fishmonger as well. And if you have a good deli nearby, order any preserved meats you want, such as sliced Parma ham, well in advance (they can slice just before you come in, and you won't have to wait when you collect them).

You'll need to contact your alcohol supplier, too, for wines of both colours, Champagne or a sparkling wine (good for buck's fizz on the big morning), brandy or rum (for the Christmas pudding butter or sauce), other spirits of choice, mixers, beers, soft drinks and waters. Choose a supplier that will deliver.

Your greengrocer will appreciate a list of what you need, and he can make up a box for you to collect at the last minute: potatoes, onions, green vegetables, etc. Try to choose seasonally, and I would always go for the organic stuff. Brussels are traditional, but don't forget about red cabbage, leeks, parsnips, fennel, sweet potatoes and Jerusalem artichokes, and all the salad leaves you will need to go with the cold meats.

Fruit and nuts should be seasonal as well: oranges and tangerines (the former for juicing and the latter for the tip of the Christmas stocking!), Cox's apples, dried figs, nuts, chestnuts and dates. Christmas is also a good time to have a little exotic fruit around too, pineapple, mango or pawpaw, for instance (these are great for breakfast).

If you have a good local baker, it might be a good idea to order some bread from him: many's the time I've gone in at the last minute and his shelves were bare!

There's quite a lot of cooking that can be done in the last couple of weeks before the holiday. You could make a Stollen (*see* page 110, wrap it well) or the marzipan for the more traditional Christmas cake (keep wrapped in the fridge). You could make up some uncooked pastry canapés, and open-freeze them: they can just be popped in the oven when you need them. And you could make and freeze a fresh cranberry sauce.

One week in advance

Check, check and double-check that everything has been organized.

This is when you could be buying everyday things that are not covered in other areas – crisps, last-minute presents, candles, crackers, Christmas paper napkins, more wrapping paper (I never buy enough).

You could make a pâté or terrine a few days before. It will last well if it is wrapped up and kept in the fridge.

You could make a royal icing for your cake a couple of days before using it, but allow two to three days after icing for it to set.

Christmas Eve

You don't want to be doing too much on Christmas Eve! This is the day for collection and delivery, from the butcher, the baker, the fishmonger, the vintner, the candlestickmaker.... So you have to make sure you or someone else is around.

If you do have to wait in for something, and you can't settle to a movie or a good book, you can still keep yourself busy. Make some mince pies or tarts or brandy snaps (they'll keep well in an airtight tin until you want to stuff them with cream); make the brandy butter or sauce, and prepare the stuffing and the giblet stock.

You could even prepare the vegetables the evening before. I know it's not ideal, but it will save you time on the day. Keep peeled potatoes and parsnips in water.

Turkey with Orange, Rosemary and Gravy

The most common mistake people make when they roast turkey is the timing, especially at Christmas. With the kids running around and the gravy boiling over, you tend to forget about it! Calculate 18 minutes per 450g (1lb). Leave the turkey to rest well before you carve it, and never use an electric carving knife, as this will rip the meat and make it tough.

Serves 10-12

1 x 4.5-5.4kg (10-12lb) turkey, giblets removed
2 oranges
24 large rosemary sprigs
55g (2oz) unsalted butter, at room temperature
coarse sea salt and freshly ground black pepper
22 streaky bacon rashers

GRAVY
600ml (1 pint) chicken stock or water
300ml (10fl oz) white wine or water
3 tbsp plain flour
2 tsp Dijon mustard

1   Preheat the oven to 190°C/375°F/gas mark 5. Wash the turkey inside and out and dry well with kitchen paper. Quarter 1 orange and put the quarters in the cavity with 2 rosemary sprigs. If you are stuffing the turkey, put the stuffing in the neck-end only, pushing it up towards the breast (don't pull the neck skin too tightly, as the stuffing expands during cooking). Secure the neck-end with skewers crossways, then tie the turkey legs together at the top of the drumsticks for a good shape.

2   Weigh the turkey and calculate the cooking time at 18 minutes per 450g (1lb). Grease a large roasting tin with a little butter. Put the turkey in the tin. Melt the remaining butter. Halve the remaining orange and squeeze one-half over the turkey, then mix the remaining juice with the melted butter. Brush some of this butter over the turkey skin and season (keep the rest for basting later). Cover the turkey with foil and roast for the calculated time. Brush it every hour with the orange-butter mixture. An hour before the end of the cooking time, remove the foil. If you want, you can bung the oven up a bit higher. The turkey is ready if the juices run clear when the thickest part of the leg is pierced with a knife

3   For each rosemary and bacon spikes, lay a bacon rasher on the work surface with a rosemary sprig on top. Wrap the bacon around the sprig and lay it on a baking sheet with the join underneath.

4   Remove the turkey from the oven and transfer it to a platter, tightly cover with foil, and allow to rest for up to 30 minutes before carving, leaving the oven on. Put the bacon and rosemary spikes in the oven 20 minutes before you are ready to serve, and cook until the bacon is crisp.

5   While the turkey is resting, pour off all but 6 tbsp of the juices from the roasting tin into a large jug and leave them to settle. When the fat has risen to the surface, spoon it off and make the darker juices underneath up to 600ml (1 pint) with water or stock, then add the wine. Heat the juices in the roasting tin on the hob. Stir in the flour, scraping up the bits from the bottom of the tin, and cook, stirring, to a nutty brown. Slowly pour in the liquid, then bring to the boil and keep stirring until thickened. Season with the mustard and salt and pepper.

6   Serve the bird with the spikes, roasties, and whatever else you want.

Roast Turkey Stuffed with Cream Cheese and Herbs

Here's a quick and easy turkey recipe that all the family are sure to love!

Serves 10-12

1 x 4.5kg (10lb) oven-ready turkey, giblets removed
1 bunch fresh parsley, stalks removed
250g (9oz) cream cheese
1 bunch fresh coriander, stalks removed
4 tbsp olive oil
salt and freshly ground black pepper

1   Preheat the oven to 180°C/350°F/gas mark 4.

2   Place the turkey on a board and carefully lift the skin up at the neck. Work your hand under it to ease it away from the breast completely.

3   Process the parsley in a blender until chopped. Add the cream cheese and gradually add the coriander, blending between each addition until smooth. Finally, add 1 tbsp of the olive oil and blend well. Alternatively, chop the herbs as finely as you can and mix with the cream cheese and 1 tbsp olive oil.

4   Press the cream mixture into the space between the breast and the skin of the turkey. Pull the skin back into place over the cheese mixture, press to re-shape and smooth over.

5   Place the turkey in a roasting tin and drizzle with the rest of the olive oil. Season well with salt and pepper, and roast for 18 minutes per 450g (1lb), or until the juices run clear when the thickest part of the leg is pierced with a knife. Baste the turkey with the pan juices after 45 minutes.

6   Cover with foil and leave to stand for 15 minutes before carving.

Roast Goose with Stuffing

I bought my first goose from a butcher's shop in Malton, called Derrick Fox, which used to have geese, turkey, rabbit and pheasant hung up outside. Goose is fantastic, but you must get a good bird or it can be as tough as old boots. Serve the roast bird with a green vegetable, potatoes roasted in the goose fat, fried apple slices, and black pudding.

Serves 6

1 x 4.5kg (10lb) goose with giblets (and any extra giblets you might get from your butcher if you ask nicely)
salt and freshly ground black pepper
about 600ml (1 pint) chicken stock
a little cornflour slaked in water
a little Marmite

STUFFING
1kg (2¼lb) good sausage-meat
1 onion, peeled and chopped
1 garlic clove, peeled and smashed
1 medium egg, beaten
freshly grated nutmeg
2 tbsp brandy

1 Preheat the oven to 220°C/425°F/gas mark 7.

2 Prick the bird all over with a fork or needle, rub generously with salt and pepper, then roast on a rack over a deep tin, starting it loosely covered with foil, for 15 minutes per 450g (1lb). From time to time, remove fat from the roasting pan and reserve. Remove the foil 30 minutes before your calculated completion time to allow the skin to brown and crisp.

3 While the bird is roasting, make the gravy. Chop up the neck, gizzard and heart, and simmer in the stock for about 2 hours, topping up with more stock or water as necessary. Strain. Boil to reduce a little if necessary, and thicken with the cornflour. Season and add Marmite to taste.

4 About 1 hour before the bird is due to come out of the oven, make the stuffing. In a large bowl, mix all the ingredients together well and then spoon the mixture into a large non-stick loaf pan. Put in the oven with the bird and leave it in there when you take the bird out.

5 When the goose is cooked through, leave it to stand for 20 minutes before attempting to carve it. Transfer it to a large chopping board and sever the legs. Cut off one breast in a single piece, then the other, reversing the bird to point the other way to make this easier. Cut through the legs at the ball-socket joint to separate them into drumsticks and thighs. Lay the breast pieces skin-side down and cut into slices across and down at a 45 degree angle. Arrange the slices on a warmed ovenproof dish. Cut slices off the legs and arrange them, skin-side up, around the breast meat. Detach the wings and cut them in half across the middle joint, slicing off what meat you can. Pick over the carcass, removing any meat that is left. Just before serving, you can flash this carved meat under the grill briefly. This will crisp up the skin as well.

6 Turn the stuffing out of its tin, and slice it like a meat loaf. Serve the goose accompanied by slices of the stuffing, and any other chosen accompaniments. Pass the gravy separately.

Brussels Sprouts with Chestnuts and Bacon

A simple way to make Brussels taste more interesting – although if you use Brussels still on the vine (much more readily available now), the sprouts don't dry out so much and are fresher in flavour. Chestnuts are readily available in cans or vacuumm-packed from delis and supermarkets. If buying a can, look carefully to make sure it is a savoury version.

Serves 10-12

1.3kg (3lb) Brussels sprouts, or 2 stems Brussels sprouts, trimmed

salt and freshly ground black pepper

a large knob of unsalted butter

12 smoked streaky bacon rashers or dry-cured ham, cut in thin matchsticks

1 x 200g pack cooked, peeled whole chestnuts (vacuum-packed)

1   Bring a large pan of salted water to the boil, add the sprouts and cook until just tender, 8-12 minutes, depending on their size. Drain well.

2   Meanwhile, melt the butter in a large frying pan or wok and fry the bacon until crisp. Add the chestnuts and cook for about a minute, to heat through.

3   When warm, tip in the drained Brussels. Mix well and season with salt and pepper.

Roast Potatoes

Everyone has a different recipe for roast potatoes, but this is mine. It was my gran's first, then my mother's, and it's still the best. Use lard or dripping for the cooking fat (or vegetable oil if you don't have either), but best of all use some goose fat.

Serves 6

10 medium King Edward, Maris
   Piper or Desirée potatoes
a good pinch of salt
50g (1¾oz) fat (*see* above)

1 Preheat the oven to 200°C/400°F/gas mark 6. Peel the potatoes and cut each one in half (into 3 if large). Place in a saucepan, cover with cold water and add the salt. Bring to the boil and simmer for a maximum of 3-4 minutes. Put into a colander and allow to drain well.

2 Heat the lard or dripping in a roasting tray on the stove, and fry the potatoes until they start to brown. Turn them occasionally. Sprinkle generously with salt, then roast for about 30 minutes.

3 Remove from the oven and turn the potatoes in the tray in order to prevent them from sticking. Roast for another 30 minutes and remove. Serve immediately. (I also love roast potatoes cold – which is why I always make bucketloads of them! I eat them with cold meat and a good wodge of butter.)

Roast Parsnips

I love these, at Christmas or any other time of the year.

Serves 6

900g (2lb) parsnips, peeled and
   quartered
2 tbsp olive oil
2 fresh thyme sprigs, leaves
   picked off
salt and freshly ground black
   pepper
40g (1½oz) unsalted butter
4-6 tbsp runny honey

1 Preheat the oven to 200°C/400°F/gas mark 6. If the parsnips are large and have woody centres, cut these out before cooking. The parsnips can be boiled in salted water for 2 minutes before roasting.

2 Preheat a roasting tray on the stove and add the oil. Fry the parsnips until golden on all sides, allowing burnt tinges on the edges. Add the thyme and roast, turning every 10 minutes, for 20-30 minutes.

3 Remove from the oven and season. Add the butter and honey. Return to the oven for 5-10 minutes. Place in a serving dish and spoon over juices.

Sausage-meat, Red Pepper and Apricot Stuffing Balls

I did this for a magazine article once, and people love them. They're so simple to prepare! All you have to do is mix the sausage-meat with a few bits of sage and other herbs, mould the mixture up into balls, and put them in the oven for 30 minutes.

Makes 16 stuffing balls

450g (1lb) good sausage-meat (or good sausages removed from their casings)
2 tbsp ground almonds
2 roasted red peppers (canned or bottled), finely chopped
8 dried apricots, finely chopped
1 tsp mixed dried herbs
olive oil

1   Place the sausage-meat in a bowl. Add the ground almonds, red peppers, apricots and herbs. Season with salt and pepper and mix well.

2   Roll into 16 balls and place on a greased baking sheet. Brush with olive oil and cook with the turkey at 180°C/350°F/gas mark 4 for the last 30 minutes. Keep warm while the turkey is resting.

Chestnut Stuffing

Stuff this into the turkey as described on page 124, or bake in a separate loaf tin.

Makes enough to stuff a 4.5-5.4kg (10-12lb) turkey

25g (1oz) unsalted butter
1 large onion, peeled and finely chopped
5 juniper berries
1kg (2¼lb) good sausage-meat (or good sausages removed from their casings)
1 x 200g pack cooked, peeled whole chestnuts (vacuum-packed), roughly chopped
2 medium eggs
4 tbsp chopped fresh sage
2 tbsp chopped fresh parsley
115g (4oz) white breadcrumbs
¼ tsp ground allspice
salt and ground black pepper

1   In a medium saucepan, melt the butter over a gentle heat, then add the onion and juniper berries. Cook for 5 minutes, without allowing the onion to colour. Leave to cool. Remove and discard the juniper berries.

2   In a large bowl, mix the onion with the rest of the ingredients. To make sure you've got the seasoning right, fry a small piece of the stuffing before shaping, then taste and adjust as necessary. (You can make the stuffing a day ahead to the end of this step and keep in the fridge until ready to use. It can also be frozen.

3   Shape into about 24 balls – this is easier with wet hands – and bake in a roasting tin with the turkey at 180°C/350°F/gas mark 4 for 35-40 minutes.

Bread Sauce

My grandmother left me an old Be-Ro flour book in her will, which had been passed down from my great-great-grandmother. In it there were alternatives and variations to classic recipes, written in pencil by my great-grandmother: the pages were full of crossings out, and notes saying that "this doesn't work". This and the following jelly are from that book.

Serves 8

225g (8oz) stale French stick
700ml (1¼ pints) full-fat milk
1 small onion, peeled and studded
    with 6 cloves
1 bay leaf
a good knob of unsalted butter
a pinch of ground allspice
about 200ml (7fl oz) double cream

1   Shave the light-brown crust from the French stick with a bread knife and discard it. Cut the bread centre into 5cm (2in) cubes. In a saucepan, bring the milk, onion, bay, butter, allspice and 3 tbsp cream to the boil. Reduce the heat, then add the bread. Gently simmer, uncovered, for 5 minutes. Add a little seasoning and then cool. Remove the onion and bay. The sauce can be refrigerated in a covered container overnight. To serve, warm through gently in a pan, adding enough double cream to give a light consistency. Grind over some black pepper and serve.

Spiced Redcurrant Jelly

Make your jelly well in advance, allowing it to set nicely.

Makes 1 litre (1¾ pints)

1kg (2¼lb) Bramley apples
1kg (2¼lb) fresh cranberries
1 tsp powdered cinnamon
granulated sugar

1   Peel and chop the apples. Put the cranberries into a large pan as they are with the apples, cinnamon and enough water to just cover. Bring to the boil and simmer until the cranberries are soft.

2   Pass the mixture through a sieve lined with a thin tea-towel, J-cloth or muslin into a measuring jug. To every 600ml (1 pint) of liquid add 500g (1lb 2oz) granulated sugar.

3   Pour the mixture back into a clean pan and cook gently until it reaches 105°C/220°F on a sugar thermometer (or when a few drops on a cold saucer begin to set within a minute or two).

4   Pour into sterilized jam jars, cover while still very hot and allow to cool and set.

Sausage and Bacon Wraps with Sage and Honey

Just look at them bubbling away in the pan: a lovely mixture of sausage and bacon. Buy dry-cured bacon so that when you fry it you don't get that weeping white liquid coming out the bacon (from the water injected into so much bacon these days). Both sausage and bacon will end up being nice and crisp and brown.

Serves 4

8 streaky bacon rashers
16 cocktail sausages
16 small fresh sage leaves
2 tbsp runny honey

1 Preheat the oven to 180°C/350°F/gas mark 4. Cut each of the bacon rashers in half.

2 Roll up the sausages in the bacon with a small sage leaf. Secure with a wooden cocktail stick if you like (it's not entirely necessary), and arrange in a shallow tin. Drizzle with the runny honey.

3 Place in the oven while the turkey or goose is resting, and cook at 180°C/350°F/gas mark 4 for 25-30 minutes. Turn over once or twice to brown evenly all over. Remove the cocktail sticks before serving, if necessary.

Christmas Pudding

Make Christmas pudding at least a month in advance – ideally in August or September – and allow it to sit in the fridge or larder like my grandmother used to, with an old fly net over the top to stop flies nibbling. I like to make this recipe in two 1.5-litre (2¾ pint) bowls rather than one large one, as I find this makes a better-tasting pudding.

Serves 10

350g (12oz) sultanas
350g (12oz) currants
150g (5½oz) dried figs, chopped
115g (4oz) mixed candied peel, chopped
100g (3½oz) dried apricots, chopped
75g (2¾oz) glacé cherries, halved
150ml (5floz) brandy (I use a good Cognac)
115g (4oz) stem ginger in syrup, chopped, plus 3 tbsp of the syrup
2 Bramley apples, peeled, cored and grated
juice and finely grated zest of 2 oranges
6 medium eggs, beaten
250g (9oz) shredded suet
350g (12oz) soft muscovado sugar
250g (9oz) fresh white breadcrumbs
200g (7oz) self-raising flour
1 tsp ground mixed spice
unsalted butter, for greasing

1 In a large bowl, soak the sultanas, currants, figs, peel, apricots and cherries in the brandy, covered, overnight if possible – or for at least a few hours.

2 In a larger bowl mix the ginger and syrup, apple, orange juice and zest, eggs, suet, sugar, breadrumbs and flour. Using a wooden spoon or your hands, stir in the soaked fruit and mixed spice and mix well.

3 Butter the bowls, and divide the mixture between them. Cover with circles of greaseproof paper with a folded pleat down the centre to allow the pudding to expand. Tie with some string and steam for 3 hours.

4 Let the puddings cool before removing the paper. Cover them with clingfilm over the top of pudding and bowl, and store in a cool, dry place if you aren't using them straight away. You can soak them with more booze in the run-up to Christmas.

5 To reheat, steam the puddings for 2 hours before turning out and flaming with hot brandy.

Quick Christmas Pudding with Baked Ice-cream

This is a great way of saving time on Christmas Day. The ice-cream parcels are better made in advance (at least the day before) and placed in the freezer. The icing sugar on the top caramelizes to create a lovely crunchy garnish for the hot Christmas pudding.

Serves 4

8 filo pastry sheets
1 medium egg, beaten
4 scoops bought or home-made
    vanilla ice-cream
icing sugar
4 x 115g small Christmas puddings
200ml (7fl oz) brandy sauce (see
    opposite)
4 fresh mint sprigs

1 Preheat the oven to 220°C/425°F/gas mark 7.

2 Unroll the filo and cut into 12 x 10cm (4in) squares. Layer 3 of the squares at slight alternate angles and brush with some beaten egg.

3 Place a scoop of the ice-cream in the centre of each filo square, and bring up the sides of the pastry to stick together. Brush with beaten egg.

4 If cooking straight away, dust with icing sugar, place on an oven tray and bake for about 3-4 minutes. Alternatively, place in the freezer until ready to use (much better).

5 Meanwhile, place the puddings in the microwave to cook (follow packet instructions) and warm the brandy sauce through on the stove.

6 Spoon the warm sauce into the centre of the plates, and place a Christmas pudding in the middle. Remove the ice-cream parcel from the oven and place on top of the pudding.

7 To finish, simply dust the top with icing sugar and garnish with a sprig of mint. Serve immediately.

Brandy Sauce

This is one of the few recipes I use granulated sugar in. As you can probably imagine, it was used in my grandmother's recipe (although she had to grate sugar from the large lump or chop sugar cubes). I remember her bringing this sauce back home to the farmhouse, and fighting with my sister to remove the greaseproof paper from the top.

Serves 4-6

200ml (7fl oz) double cream
600ml (1 pint) full-fat milk
25g (1oz) cornflour, slaked with
  4 tbsp cold water
55g (2oz) unrefined granulated
  sugar
55g (2oz) unsalted butter, cubed
brandy, to taste

1 Bring the cream and milk to the boil together, and then stir in the slaked cornflour. Bring back to the boil, stirring, to thicken.

2 Remove from the heat and stir in the sugar and butter, until dissolved. Finally, stir in brandy to taste.

3 Cover to stop a skin forming, and keep warm.

Christmas Pudding Ice-cream

This is a simple way of using leftover Christmas pudding. Please invest in a decent ice-cream maker, which blends while it is freezing. Make sure Father Christmas comes down the chimney with one! Serve the ice-cream with a large glass of brandy and brandy snaps.

Serves 4-6

85g (3oz) leftover Christmas
  pudding, chopped into small
  pieces
2 tbsp brandy
140g (5oz) caster sugar
1 cinnamon stick
½ tsp ground mixed spice
225ml (8fl oz) custard base for
  ice-cream (*see* page 151)
150ml (5fl oz) double cream

1 Soak the Christmas pudding in the brandy.

2 To make the stock syrup, heat 150ml (5fl oz) water and the sugar together in a heavy-based pan until the sugar has melted, then simmer to reduce to 185ml (6½fl oz). Transfer to a small pan and add the cinnamon stick and mixed spice. Remove from the heat and leave to cool and infuse for 15 minutes.

3 Mix the custard with the cream. Strain the stock syrup to remove the cinnamon and add to the cream mixture. Mix in the Christmas pudding and brandy.

4 Churn in an ice-cream maker until thick and frozen, then transfer to a freezerproof container. Store in the freezer for up to a couple of weeks.

NEW YEAR'S DAY

No-one wants to be slaving away in the kitchen with a hang-over on New Year's Day, so you have two choices: make it easy or make sure you can prepare most of it in advance. Oh yes, and of course the food must feel special. Everything in this chapter fits that criteria!

Bloody Mary

The ultimate hangover cure! Make your own tomato juice or use tomato passata. The only other things you need are plenty of Tabasco, a good wedge of lemon and, most importantly, loads of ice cubes. That way you get the Bloody Mary chilled right down, which is perfect for those mornings after the night before.

Serves 1 (I like it strong!)

50ml (2fl oz) vodka
90ml (3fl oz) tomato juice (*see* above)
juice of ½ lemon
2-4 dashes Tabasco sauce
3 dashes Worcestershire sauce
freshly ground black pepper
ice cubes
1 lemon wedge

1 Place the vodka, tomato and lemon juices, Tabasco and Worcestershire sauces in a blender or a cocktail shaker and mix. Taste and season with black pepper and/or more of either sauce if needed.

2 Pour into a tall glass full of ice, and serve with the wedge of lemon on top of the glass.

Scrambled Eggs with Chilli and Crisp Streaky Bacon on Toast

Scrambled egg is so simple to make, but still people overcook it and end up with rubbery, gelatinized stuff on toast. To prevent this, add double cream halfway through the cooking while you whisk everything together in the pan. Be sure to use dry-cured bacon.

Serves 4

12 streaky bacon rashers
55g (2oz) unsalted butter
6 medium eggs, beaten
salt and ground black pepper
100ml (3½fl oz) double cream

TO SERVE

4 pieces sliced bread, toasted and buttered
1 green chilli, seeded and finely diced

1 Heat a sauté pan on a medium heat. Add the bacon with half the butter, and cook until crisp and golden brown, a few minutes only. Remove from the pan and keep warm.

2 Wipe the pan and return to the heat with the remaining butter. Season the eggs well with salt and pepper, then pour into the pan. Quickly mix the eggs with a whisk and, when half-cooked, add the cream, whisking all the time.

3 Just as the eggs are beginning to set, remove from the heat, and season again. Spoon on to the toast, with a scattering of chopped chilli on top and bacon on the side. Serve immediately.

Smoked Haddock with Poached Egg and Horseradish Mash

Most people don't think poached eggs can be prepared in advance, but they can: simply poach the egg, then place it into ice-cold water to cool down. When cold, pop it in the fridge. When you want the eggs, blanch them in boiling water for 30 seconds and place them on your haddock. This is particularly useful when serving breakfast for lots of people.

Serves 4

4 x 200g (7oz) pieces natural
   smoked haddock
850ml (1½ pints) full-fat milk
juice of 1 lemon
6 black peppercorns
a few fresh parsley stalks
salt and freshly ground black
   pepper
4 large eggs
150g (5½oz) fresh young spinach
   leaves, washed

HORSERADISH MASH
900g (2lb) King Edward or Maris
   Piper potatoes, peeled and
   chopped
100g (3½oz) unsalted butter
approx 200ml (7fl oz) full-fat
   milk, warmed
2 tbsp creamed horseradish

1   For the mash, cook the potatoes in boiling salted water until tender, about 15 minutes. Once cooked, drain well and, while hot but not wet, place back in the pan and return to the heat. Mash with the butter and the warm milk. Once you get the texture you want, beat in the horseradish and some salt and pepper to taste and keep warm.

2   For the haddock, put the milk, lemon juice, peppercorns, parsley stalks and a little salt into a medium-sized flat pan, and bring to a simmer. At the same time, place a pan of salted water on to boil for the eggs.

3   Add the haddock pieces to the simmering milk, and cook gently for about 6-8 minutes. While this is cooking, crack the eggs into the stirred rapidly boiling water, and poach for 2-3 minutes. In another medium pan, quickly wilt the spinach in only the water clinging to the leaves. Season.

4   Place the spinach, then the mash, on the plates. Drain the haddock and place on the mash. I spoon a little of the flavoured milk over this and top with a soft poached egg.

Grilled Aubergine with Tomato Sauce

Aubergines are not really English, but I'm growing them in my greenhouse and they taste wonderful. Simply pan-fry slices of aubergine, top with mozzarella cheese and Parmesan, place under the grill and serve with a tomato sauce. This is a real classic Italian dish that we Brits have learned to love.

Serves 4

plain white flour
4 medium eggs, beaten with a
    pinch of salt
2 aubergines, cut into 8mm (³/₈ in)
    rounds
olive oil
salt and ground black pepper
300g (10¹/₂ oz) buffalo mozzarella,
    sliced
100g (3¹/₂ oz) Parmesan, grated

TOMATO AND BASIL SAUCE
extra virgin olive oil
1 medium onion, peeled and finely
    chopped
2 garlic cloves, peeled and finely
    chopped
1kg (2¹/₄ lb) tomatoes, diced
¹/₄ tsp dried oregano
8 fresh basil leaves, torn

1 To make the sauce, heat 4 tbsp of olive oil in a pan and fry the onion and garlic for 4-5 minutes. Add the tomatoes and oregano, bring to the boil, then reduce the heat and cook for 10-15 minutes. Halfway through the cooking, add the basil leaves. Season and blend to a smooth sauce, then leave to one side.

2 Preheat 2 frying pans on the stove, and preheat the grill.

3 Put the flour and beaten eggs in separate shallow bowls. Dip the aubergine slices first in flour and then in beaten egg, and fry in shallow olive oil until golden on both side. Put each slice on absorbent paper.

4 Place the drained aubergine slices on a grill tray and season. Top with the sliced mozzarella and grated Parmesan.

5 Grill until the cheeses have melted and started to brown, then serve immediately with the heated tomato and basil sauce.

Honey-glazed Ham with Spiced Apple and Cider

I remember queuing up at Scotts Butchers as a kid with my gran and auntie. Armed with their handbags and pensions every Thursday, they would wait for dry-cured smoked back bacon and York ham. Sadly they don't do York ham any more, but if you're in York it's worth going to Scotts on Petergate to experience one of the greatest pork suppliers there is.

Serves 4-6

1 x 3.5kg (7.5lb) boiled ham,
   cooled
115g (4oz) clear honey
1 tbsp English mustard
finely grated zest and juice of
   1 orange
20 cloves

APPLE SAUCE
500g (1lb 2oz) Bramley Seedling
   apples
25g (1oz) butter
2 tbsp cider
¼ tsp freshly grated nutmeg
¼ tsp powdered cinnamon
¼ tsp freshly ground black pepper
25g (1 oz) soft dark brown sugar

1 Preheat the oven to 220°C/425°F/gas mark 7.

2 Score the ham fat diagonally at 2.5cm (1in) intervals, first in one direction, then another, to produce a diamond pattern.

3 Mix the honey, mustard, orange zest and enough orange juice to make a spreadable mixture. Smear this glaze over the ham. Stud the ham with the cloves at the points of the diamond shapes. Bake for 30 minutes, or until cooked through.

5 Meanwhile, for the sauce, peel, core and cut up the apples. Put them in a pan with all the remaining sauce ingredients apart from the sugar. Cover and cook until soft enough to beat to a purée. Add sugar to taste, and more spices if you like.

6 Serve the ham in slices, hot or cold, with the apple sauce.

Salmon with Beetroot, Cauliflower and Horseradish Cream

An odd dish, I know, but all the flavours work really well when eaten together. You can serve it all cold, but I like the vegetables cold and the salmon hot from the pan.

Serves 4

1 large cauliflower
juice of 1 lemon
4 tbsp horseradish cream
150ml (5fl oz) double cream, par-whipped
salt and freshly ground black pepper
4 x 115-175g (4-6oz) salmon fillets, skin on
olive oil

BEETROOT
8 medium beetroots, cooked
4 shallots, peeled and chopped
1 garlic clove, peeled and chopped
75ml (2½fl oz) extra virgin olive oil
10g (¼oz) mixed fresh chives, parsley and dill, chopped
2 tbsp balsamic vinegar

1 To prepare the beetroots, peel them, cut them into segments and place these in a bowl.

2 Sweat the shallots and garlic in a pan in a little of the oil, with no colour, then leave to cool. Mix with the herbs, balsamic and remaining oil, pour over the beetroot and leave to one side.

3 Divide the cauliflower into small florets and cook these in boiling water for about 5 minutes. When just cooked, plunge into iced water, drain and leave to one side.

4 Make the horseradish cream by combining the lemon juice and horseradish, then adding the par-whipped cream and some seasoning. Fold in the cauliflower and place in a serving bowl.

5 Season the salmon, then cook it in a hot pan in a little oil, for 3-4 minutes on both sides.

6 Serve the cold beetroot and cauliflower in separate containers on a plate, and the hot salmon on top of either one and the horseradish cream on the side.

Pan-fried Cod with Peas, Pancetta and Sweet Potato Crisp

This is probably the most cheffy recipe in the book, but it tastes great. The most important thing is to use a great cod fillet – thick white flesh with the skin still on – as this will help hold it together while cooking.

Serves 4

4 x 175-200g (6-7oz) thick pieces
   cod fillet, skin on
olive oil
salt and freshly ground black
   pepper
unsalted butter
200g (7oz) warm mashed potato
   (*see* page 143, omitting the
   horseradish)
8 slices pancetta, grilled until crisp
4 thin strips sweet potato,
   deep-fried

SAUCE
400ml (14fl oz) chicken stock
55g (2oz) pancetta, diced
15g (1oz) unsalted butter
1 small onion, peeled and
   finely chopped
2 garlic cloves, peeled and
   crushed
2 tbsp horseradish cream
a dash of white wine
150ml (5fl oz) double cream
350g (12oz) frozen peas
a pinch of caster sugar

1 Preheat the oven to 200°C/400°F/gas mark 6.

2 Start the sauce by reducing the stock. Boil until you have about 50ml (2fl oz) left.

3 Sauté the diced pancetta in the butter until crisp, then add the onion and garlic and soften without allowing them to colour. Add the horseradish, wine and reduced stock and simmer for a few minutes. Add the cream, peas and sugar, stir and season, and simmer for a few more minutes to heat the peas through.

4 Brush the cod fillets with olive oil, season and pan-fry for a minute on each side. Finish by cooking for 10 minutes in the oven, or until cooked,

5 Place the warm mash in the centre of the plates with the cod. Put a slice of crisp pancetta and a sweet-potato crisp on top, and spoon the sauce around.

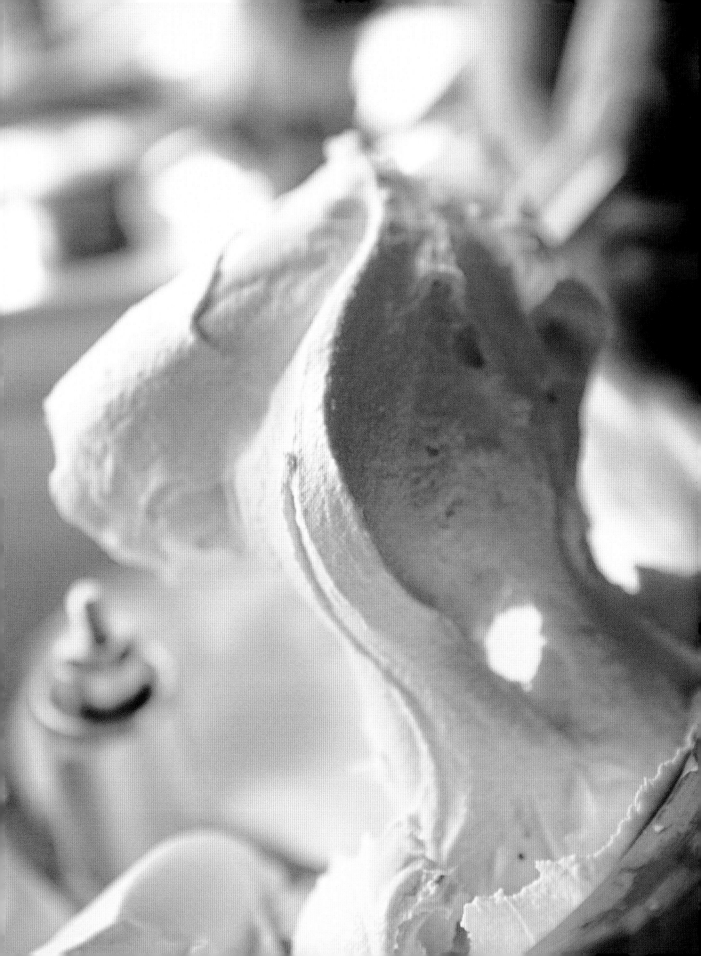

Ginger and Butternut Squash Ice-cream

I know what you're thinking, squash in an ice-cream? Sounds weird, but trust me: I won't let you down. It really is a delight!

Serves 6

450ml (16fl oz) double cream
2 tbsp peeled and chopped fresh
    root ginger
4 medium egg yolks
100g (3½oz) caster sugar
ice
150g (5½oz) cooked, cooled and
    puréed butternut squash
a dash of lemon juice

1 Bring the cream and ginger to the boil together. Cover, remove from the heat and leave to steep for 30 minutes.

2 Return the cream to the boil. Whisk together the egg yolks and sugar in a jug and pour in some of the hot cream mixture. Mix quickly, then pour into the cream mixture left in the pan. Continue cooking over a gentle heat for 3-4 minutes, or until the mixture coats the back of the spoon. Cool over ice, stirring occasionally, until cold.

3 Mix the cooked and cooled squash purée into the cooled custard, add lemon juice to taste, and strain through a fine sieve. Freeze in an ice-cream machine or in a freezerproof container. Keep frozen until ready to use.

PARTIES, GIFTS AND TREATS

I love a wide variety of food at parties – from the traditional stuff like sausage rolls to crackers with some good cheese and a little onion marmalade to nibbles like home-made pork scratchings or spicy nuts. But of course the one thing no winter party should be without is a good glass of mulled wine!

Sweet Kir Royale

This is one of the best pre-dinner drinks. It's this drink and Parma ham wrapped around thin, home-made bread sticks that I remember most about my hols a few years ago in Italy. Although a much cheaper option is to drink this while watching *Corrie*!

Serves 6

6 tbsp crème de cassis
6 brown sugar cubes
1 bottle Champagne,
   or sparkling wine

1 Place a tablespoon of crème de cassis in each of the Champagne glasses along with a brown sugar cube.

2 Open the Champagne carefully and pour it into the glasses at a 45-degree angle. Serve immediately.

Mulled Wine

Mulled wine is great served anywhere, especially when the nights are drawing in and you want something to really knock that sore throat on the head.

Serves 8-10, depending on how thirsty you are...

3 bottles red wine
2 oranges, zest peeled with a
   peeler, then juiced
2 lemons, zest peeled with a
   peeler
2 vanilla pods, split
1 cinnamon stick
900g (2lb) caster sugar
3 cloves
4 juniper berries
1 bay leaf

1 Simply chuck everything into a pot with 1 litre (1¾ pint) water, bring it to the boil, and leave to infuse for 10 minutes to infuse.

2 Serve warm.

Mulled wine infusing in a saucepan.

Melted Vacherin Mont d'Or
with New Potatoes and Smoked Duck

Vacherin is a classic French cheese. You can serve it as you would Brie or Camembert, but when baked in its box it makes a fondue-like dish – and we Brits love a fondue!

Serves 2-4

1 Vacherin Mont d'Or in a box

TO SERVE
200g (7oz) smoked duck, sliced
100g (3½oz) cooked new potatoes
55g (2oz) small gherkins
½ loaf crusty bread, broken up

1   Preheat the oven to 220°C/425°F/gas mark 7. Wrap the box of cheese in foil around the edge to stop it from burning. Place on a baking tray and put into the oven for 15 minutes, until warm and melting in the middle.

2   Serve hot in the centre of a serving plate with the sliced duck, the potatoes, gherkins and torn bread around the edge.

Hot Spiced Nuts

My sister once picked up some nuts in a pub, chewed on them for about half an hour, then spat them out, bemused only to discover they were olive stones. (Sorry sis!)

Serves 4-6

55g (2oz) unsalted butter
175g (6oz) mixed nuts
½ tsp each of dried chilli flakes, medium curry powder, cayenne pepper and ground ginger
5 tbsp soft brown sugar
2 tbsp chopped fresh parsley

1   Preheat the oven to 220°C/425°F/gas mark 7. Melt the butter in a large sauté pan and sauté the nuts over a gentle heat for 3-4 minutes. Add the chilli flakes, curry powder, cayenne, ginger and sugar and cook for another 3-4 minutes.

2   Pour the nut mixture into an oven tray and dust with salt to taste. Stir and roast for 5 minutes. Stir in the parsley and serve warm.

Hot spiced nuts.

Melted Vacherin Mont d'Or.

Pork Scratchings

It's nice to offer your own scratchings with pre-dinner drinks, or you can even use them as a starter for a meal.

Makes as many as you like!

pork rind (preferably from the loin)
fine salt

1 Cut any excess fat from underneath the pork rind.

2 Preheat the oven to 200°C/400°F/gas mark 6.

3 Instead of scoring the rind, cut into 5mm (¼in) strips, then sprinkle with salt. Bake for 30-40 minutes (or longer for thicker pieces), until the pieces become crunchy.

Grissini and Dips

This is a quick and simple party idea, hardly a recipe, and it's good for a mobile starter to a dinner party, too

Makes as many as you like!

thin breadsticks or grissini
selection of dips, perhaps
    including garlic mayonnaise, soft
    cheese and tapenade
toasted sesame or poppy seeds or
    fresh herbs, finely chopped

1 Dip the ends of the breadsticks or grissini in the garlic mayonnaise, soft cheese or tapenade. Then dip the dipped end of the stick into the toasted seeds or herbs.

2 Serve, dipped end up, in tall glasses or in a large jug, so people can dive in and help themselves.

3 Alternatively, you can just wrap the grissini in some Parma ham, which makes a great snack as well.

Sausage Rolls

For me, party food wouldn't be party food without sausage rolls. I always look with horror at the rows and rows of sausage rolls and vol-au-vents stuffed with mushrooms and prawns with Marie Rose sauce at wedding buffets. There are no prawn vol-au-vents in this book and there won't ever be in any of my books, as I think they are the most repulsive things to ever hit the plate! However, sausage rolls when made right and served warm can be the finest delight England has to offer. You can use ordinary sausage-meat for these, either from a packet or meat taken out of the skins of your favourite sausages. But my favourite is wild boar sausage-meat, which makes a very special sausage roll!

Makes 16–20

450g (1lb) wild-boar sausage-meat
finely grated zest of ½ lemon
1 heaped tsp each of chopped
   fresh thyme and sage
salt and freshly ground black
   pepper
225g (8oz) ready-made puff pastry
plain flour
1 egg yolk mixed with 2 tsp milk

1 Preheat the oven to 200°C/400°F/gas mark 6.

2 Mix together the sausage-meat, lemon zest and chopped herbs. Season with salt and pepper. This can now be refrigerated, covered, to firm while the pastry is being rolled.

3 Roll the pastry to about 3mm (⅛in) thick on a floured surface. Cut into 3 long strips approximately 10cm (4in) wide.

4 The sausage-meat can now be moulded, using your hands, into 3 long sausages, preferably 2.5cm (1in) thick. If the meat is too moist, then dust it with flour.

5 Sit each "sausage" on a pastry strip, 2-3cm (¾-1¼in) from the edge of the pastry. Brush the pastry along the other side, close to the sausage, with the egg yolk and milk mixture. Fold the pastry over the meat, rolling it as you do so. When the pastry meets, leave a small overlap before cutting away any excess. Once rolled all along, lift them carefully, making sure that the seal is on the base when put down.

6 These can now be transferred to a greased baking sheet. The sausage rolls can be left as they are, or you can make 3-4 cuts with scissors along the top. Brush each with the remaining egg yolk before baking for 20-30 minutes.

7 Once baked golden and crispy, remove from the oven and serve the sausage rolls warm.

Baby Coffee Eclairs

This is the kind of party food that always impresses: delicious éclairs packed with thick pastry cream.

Makes 60–70 éclairs

1 quantity choux pastry (see opposite)
1 beaten egg

COFFEE PASTRY CREAM
300ml (½ pint) whole milk
10g (¼oz) freshly ground coffee
4 large egg yolks
60g (2¼oz) unrefined caster sugar
60g (2¼oz) plain white flour, sifted
300ml (½ pint) double cream, lightly whipped

ICING
5 tsp instant coffee
3 tbsp boiling water
about 250g (9oz) fondant icing sugar

1   Preheat the oven to 220°C/425°F/gas mark 7. Lightly grease two baking sheets. Spoon the choux pastry into a large piping bag fitted with a 1.5cm (⅝in) nozzle. Pipe the pastry on the baking sheets into 4cm (1¾in) long éclairs. Brush with beaten egg and refine the shape at the same time. Bake for 15-20 minutes, or until well risen and golden.

2   Once the éclairs are fully formed and golden, turn the oven down to 160°C/ 325°/gas mark 3 and cook the éclairs for a further 5-10 minutes to dry them out until they are very crisp. The crisper they are, the easier they are to pipe and ice. Remove from the oven and cool completely – don't store them in an airtight container as this makes the pastry soggy.

3   Meanwhile, make the pastry cream: bring the milk and ground coffee to the boil in a pan, stirring all the time. Remove from the heat and leave to infuse for 10 minutes.

4   Meanwhile, whisk the egg yolks and sugar together. Add the flour and mix well. Strain the milk and coffee mixture through a fine sieve on to the egg and sugar mixture and stir well. Return to the pan and bring to the boil slowly, stirring all the time in a figure of eight so it doesn't catch. Once boiling, remove from the heat and pour into a clean bowl. Cover with cling film and leave to cool.

5   Whisk the cooled coffee pastry cream to loosen and break it down, then add the whipped cream and whisk together. Spoon into a piping bag fitted with a 5mm (¼in) nozzle. Using a little knife, make small incisions in the base of each éclair large enough to fit the nozzle. Pipe the coffee cream into the éclairs one by one, until they feel heavy and full.

6   For the icing, mix together the instant coffee and boiling water, then gradually add enough fondant icing sugar to make an icing of coating consistency. Dip each éclair into the icing one at a time and smooth off with your finger. Leave to set for 15 minutes and then serve piled high.

Choux Pastry

Don't be put off making choux pastry by rumours of it being difficult. It's not that hard – honest – and well worth it!

Makes enough for about 70 baby éclairs

115g (4oz) unsalted butter, cubed
a pinch of sugar
a pinch of salt
140g (5oz) plain white flour, sifted
3-4 eggs, beaten

1   Bring the butter and 300ml (½ pint) of cold water to the boil in a pan. Add the sugar and salt, and then immediately add the flour and beat well until the mixture comes away from the pan. Allow to cool completely (more egg is absorbed when the mixture is cold).

2   Gradually add 3 of the beaten eggs to the cooled pastry, a little at a time (it's best to do this in a food mixer or food processor) and then beat small amounts of the last egg into the mixture until you get the right consistency. The reason for only adding 3 eggs at the start is that the mixture needs to be quite tight; if you add too much egg, the end product will not rise correctly and, of course, you can always add the extra egg but you can't take it out. If the paste is to be used for fritters or *beignets*, then it has to be fairly tight. The finished paste should just fall off the paddle on the machine. It's best to use choux dough straight away, but it will keep for a couple of days in the fridge.

Chocolate Truffles

Dark-chocolate truffles, like these, are the quickest and simplest to make. Milk and white chocolate truffles need different chocolate, as dark sets more solid – increase the amount by 115g (4oz). Mine are coated in cocoa powder. You can use icing sugar, coconut or grated chocolate, but if you do, roll the truffles in the coating while the chocolate is wet.

Makes 20-30

300ml (10fl oz) double cream
300g (10½oz) 70% dark chocolate
25ml (1fl oz) rum, brandy, etc.
    (optional)

COATING
200g (7oz) 70% dark chocolate,
    broken into small pieces
55g (2oz) good cocoa powder

1 Place the cream in a pan and heat until hot, but do not boil.

2 Break the chocolate into small even pieces and place in a bowl. When the cream is hot, pour it slowly on to the chocolate and, using a whisk, mix well until all the cream is combined and the chocolate has melted.

3 Before you set this mix, add any rum or brandy, if using, then leave it to set for about 2 hours in the fridge.

4 Using a melon scoop dipped in hot water, spoon the mixture into balls. Place them on a tray and put them back into the fridge.

5 Melt the chocolate for the coating in a bowl over a pan of hot water. Then stab each truffle with a fork, using it to dip the truffle in the chocolate and roll it in the cocoa. Place it on a plate and, once you have coated all the truffles, put them back in the fridge to set.

Coffee "Mushrooms"

I invented this dish while working as a pastry chef at Chewton Glen. The guests there used to go on mushroom hunts, and bring back their booty, which was a great way of stocking the fridges and freezers with mushrooms – and the hotel guests had done all the work! This dessert seemed to suit the occasion!

Serves 4

600ml (1 pint) good coffee
  ice-cream, slightly softened
250g (9oz) 50-70% dark chocolate
good cocoa powder
icing sugar, sifted

FOR THE *TUILES*
115g (4oz) unsalted butter,
  softened
140g (5oz) icing sugar
3 medium egg whites
115g (4oz) plain flour

FOR THE COFFEE SAUCE
1 tbsp instant coffee
2 tbsp caster sugar
125ml (4fl oz) double cream

1 Preheat the oven to 200°C/400°F/gas mark 6.

2 To start the "stalks" of the mushrooms, take 4 large and 4 small dariole mounds and line them with clingfilm. Fill with the softened ice-cream and re-freeze until set hard again.

3 Prepare templates for the *tuiles* using 2 margarine tub lids. Cut a large circular hole in 1 lid and a small circlular hole in the other. Cream the butter and sugar together. Slowly add the egg whites to the mix, then fold in the flour. Place the templates on a baking tray, spread the *tuile* mix over the holes with a palette knife, then lift off the templates, leaving perfect circles. You need 4 of each size.

4 Bake for 2-3 minutes, until lightly coloured around the edges. Remove and place each disc of *tuile* over an eggcup or similar until cold. The soft *tuiles* will fold over into mushroom-cap shapes and become crisp.

5 To make the sauce, place the coffee and sugar in a teacup and add a little boiling water to dissolve to a very heavy syrup. Pour the cream into a bowl, then pour coffee on to it to colour and flavour it.

6 Grate the chocolate and scatter the gratings in a circle around the edges of the plates. Spoon the coffee sauce into the middle. Unmould the ice-creams, removing the cling film, and stand these "stalks" upright, one of each size on each plate, in the centre of the pool of sauce.

7 Turn the *tuiles* dome-side up, dust with the cocoa powder and icing sugar in a small sieve, and place the small mushroom "caps" on the small mushroom "stalks"; the large "caps" on the large "stalks". Serve the coffee mushrooms immediately.

Festive Marrons Glacés

Marrons glacés are crystallized chestnuts, and if you don't want to just devour them out of the jar, here is something to do with them for party dessert.

Serves 4

300ml (10fl oz) double cream
a dash of whisky
a dash of Grand Marnier
25g (1oz) vanilla sugar (*see* below)
12 marrons glacés in syrup
25g (1oz) dark chocolate, grated
4 fresh mint sprigs

1 Whip the double cream until almost stiff. Add the whisky, Grand Marnier and a little of the vanilla sugar to taste.

2 Using 2 tablespoons dipped in hot water, spoon the cream on to the plates in rugby-ball shapes, 3 per plate. Place the marrons glacés on the side, 3 per plate, and drizzle over some of the syrup.

3 Drizzle the remaining sugar over the top along with the grated chocolate, garnish with a sprig of mint, and serve.

Vanilla Sugar

I can never understand when walking around supermarkets why people would want to buy prepared vanilla sugar, as it is so simple to make. You could easily sell it at a farmers' market for a quid – or if you are more charitable, you could give it as presents. Otherwise, use it in desserts, and it's great in coffee.

Makes 500g (1lb 2oz)

3 good vanilla pods (Bourbon are
   great)
500g (1lb 2oz) caster sugar

1 Chop the vanilla into pieces with a knife, and place in a blender with 100g (3½ oz) of the sugar. Blend to break up the pieces.

2 Add the rest of the sugar and store in glass jars.

Fruit and Nut Biscotti

I end up making biscotti once a week because my PA devours half the jar every other week and the builders nick the rest. Biscotti are great biscuits that are easily made, and they can be stored in jars, given away as gifts, or even hung on the Christmas tree. Kids love them, as do adults, and my granny adored them.

Makes 40-50 biscotti

250g (9oz) plain flour
250g (9oz) caster sugar
½ tbsp baking powder
3 medium eggs, lightly beaten
55g (2oz) plump sultanas
55g (2oz) dried cherries
55g (2oz) pitted dates, chopped
75g (2¾oz) shelled pistachio nuts
55g (2oz) whole blanched
   almonds
55g (2oz) shelled hazelnuts
finely grated zest of 1 lemon

1   Preheat the oven to 180°C/350°F/gas mark 4.

2   Mix the flour, sugar and baking powder in a large bowl. Add half the beaten eggs and mix well, then add half of what's left and mix again. Now add the last quarter a little bit at a time, mixing, until the dough takes shape but isn't too wet (you may not need to use all the egg). Add the fruit, nuts and lemon zest and mix well.

3   Divide the dough into six and roll each sixth into a sausage shape about 2.5cm (1in) in diameter. Place, at least 6cm (2½in) apart, on baking parchment on baking trays. Wetting your hands when rolling these out helps to prevent the dough sticking.

4 Lightly flatten the "sausages" and bake until golden brown, about 20-30 minutes. Remove from the oven and leave for 10 minutes to cool and firm up. Drop the temperature of the oven to 140°C/275°F/gas mark 1.

5   With a serrated knife, cut the biscotti on an angle into 5mm (¼in) slices and lay these on the baking trays. Return to the oven and cook for 12 minutes. Turn the biscotti over and cook until they are pale golden, about 10-15 minutes.

6   When ready, remove from the oven and cool on cake racks. Store in airtight jars.

Madeleines

These little bun-textured, scallop-shaped cakes are fabulous around Christmas time. Give them away as a gift, put them on the tree like biscotti, or dip them fresh in the mulled wine on page 154.

**Makes 12 large or
24 small sponges**

2 large eggs, at room temperature
75g (2½oz) unrefined caster sugar
85g (3oz) plain white flour
1½ tsp baking powder
85g (3oz) unsalted butter, melted
1 tbsp clear honey
unrefined icing sugar, sifted

1   Preheat the oven to 190°C/375°F/gas mark 5. Butter 12 large madeleine moulds or 24 small moulds thoroughly. If you don't have madeleine moulds you can use patty tins.

2   Place the eggs and sugar in a mixing bowl and, using an electric whisk, beat on a moderate speed until thick and foamy. Sift together the flour and baking powder and then sprinkle this mixture over the egg mixture and carefully fold it in. Do *not* overwork it! Mix together the butter and honey and carefully fold this in, too.

3   Spoon the madeleine mixture into a large piping bag fitted with a 1cm (½in) plain nozzle and pipe it into the moulds. Dip your finger into a little cold water and slightly press the mixture down.

4   Bake for about 8 minutes for the small moulds or 10 minutes for the large ones, or until well risen and golden brown. You may find that the centres rise up a little; don't worry – this is quite normal.

5   Turn out on to a cooling rack and dust with a little unrefined icing sugar. You can even dip the ends into melted extra-bitter chocolate.

Mint Jelly

My grandmother was never a lover of mint jelly: she couldn't understand why you put apples in there, and her mint sauce was simply some Sarson's vinegar, a little sugar, some salt and chopped mint from the garden. But for me, mint jelly is a classic, great with any number of dishes. It needs to be made with apples to allow it to set, but it's simple to make.

Makes 450g (1lb)

1.8kg (4lb) cooking apples
55g (2oz) chopped fresh mint, including stalks, plus 2 tbsp finely chopped mint leaves
juice and finely grated zest of 1 lemon
1 tbsp white wine vinegar
approx. 675g (1½lb) caster sugar

1   Chop the apples coarsely, including the cores, and put them in a pan with the 55g (2oz) chopped mint, including stalks, the lemon zest and juice and the vinegar. Barely cover with about 1.2 litres (2 pints) cold water. Bring to the boil, turn down the heat and simmer gently for 45 minutes.

2   The proper piece of kit for the next stage is a jelly bag, but if you don't have one you could improvise. Line a colander with a double thickness of fine muslin and scald with boiling water to sterilize. Put this over a bowl, pour the contents of the pan into it and leave to drip overnight. Don't try and hurry this process by pushing with a spoon or squeezing the bag, as this will force solids through and make the jelly cloudy.

3   The next day, measure the juice and put it into a pan with 450g (1lb) caster sugar per 600ml (1 pint) of apple juice. Bring to the boil slowly, then increase the heat and boil rapidly for about 8 minutes. Continue to boil for another 2 minutes, when the right amount of water will have evaporated and the frothing boil will have changed to a thicker rolling boil, with fat bubbles plopping noisily to the surface. At this stage the setting point should have been reached.

4   Remove from the heat, pour through a sieve into a warmed jug and then stir in the remaining finely chopped mint leaves. Test by putting a spoonful of the mix on a cold plate. The surface should set as it cools and will wrinkle when prodded. Pour immediately into warm sterilized jars. Don't tilt them until set. Put on sterilized lids and keep in a cool cupboard. Once opened, keep in the fridge.

Onion Marmalade

This is bang in season around winter, and what could be better than a jar of onion marmalade given away as a gift? It goes brilliantly with melted cheese on toast, steak, roast fish, and a huge variety of other things, either hot or cold.

Makes 450g (1lb)

1.8kg (4lb) brown onions, peeled and thinly sliced
100ml (3½fl oz) olive oil
1 tbsp chopped fresh thyme
175g (6oz) caster sugar
150ml (5fl oz) red wine
6 tbsp red wine vinegar
salt and freshly ground black pepper

1   Place the onions in a large, heavy-based saucepan with the olive oil and thyme and cook over a moderate heat for 5 minutes. It is important not to let the onions brown at this stage or they will become bitter. Lower the heat, cover with a lid and cook for 20 minutes.

2   Remove the lid and add the sugar, wine, vinegar and some seasoning. Continue to cook, stirring from time to time, for about 20-30 minutes.

3   Once the jam is sticky, spoon it into sterilized jars. Lightly cover the surface with olive oil and put on the lids. Keep in a cool place until ready to use. Once opened, store in the fridge.

Index

Acknowledgements

Thanks to Simon, Catherine, Karen and Nicky for a great shoot!